W9-DJH-352

PRAISE FOR *DOG MEDICINE*

"Anyone who has ever opened their heart and asked an animal to teach them how to live—and there are so many of us—will be deeply moved by the story of Julie Barton and her soulmate Bunker. In this honest, gloriously unselfconscious and compelling memoir, she does great honor, not only to her dog, but to the miracles made possible when logic, and even language, is not allowed to stand in the way of love."

— PAM HOUSTON, AUTHOR OF *SIGHT HOUND*

"*Dog Medicine* is the kind of memoir that will bring tears of sadness and joy to anyone who has ever felt rescued by a pet. It is about how the right animal can inspire not just hope but mercy. Julie Barton's prose is lyrical and unflinching, a gorgeous howl in the darkness that leads the reader into the light."

— STEVE ALMOND, AUTHOR OF *CANDYFREAK*

"*Dog Medicine* accomplishes what only the most authentic writing can do: craft language so that readers live an experience. In this brilliant and lyrical debut memoir, Barton has written a narrative of inescapable appeal. The bond, here, between human and animal isn't easy or sentimental—rather, it's archetypal and magical. There is a Buddhist story of a Bodhisattva, an enlightened one, who refused to enter paradise until an ailing companion dog could also enter. *Dog Medicine* relates an equally powerful story of devotion, only related in real, worldly terms with heartbreaking consequences and rewards."

— SUE WILLIAM SILVERMAN, AUTHOR OF *THE PAT BOONE FAN CLUB: MY LIFE AS A WHITE ANGLO-SAXON JEW*

"There are times when another creature can hold our love until we can hold it for ourselves. And then, in perfect symbiosis, the beloved can become the lover, until they are one force. *Dog Medicine* shows us that this is not just possible, but sometimes, a matter of life or death."

— LAURA MUNSON, *NEW YORK TIMES* BESTSELLING AUTHOR OF
THIS IS NOT THE STORY YOU THINK IT IS

"Julie Barton's memoir *Dog Medicine* is the most heartbreaking and heartwarming book I've read in years. It tells both the harrowing story of a depression so severe that Barton felt it might 'vaporize her into millions of tiny molecules' and the consoling story of her eventual recovery through the love of and for her beloved dog and 'spirit twin,' Bunker. Reader, this book about how Barton's dog changed her life will change your life."

— DAVID JAUSS, AUTHOR OF *GLOSSOLALIA:*
NEW & SELECTED STORIES

"You may think you're about to read a book about a charming dog, or about struggling with identity in your twenties, or about how a young woman pulls herself together after a diagnosis of depression. But you'd be wrong. *Dog Medicine* is a love story—a great, big, beautiful, honest, touching, intoxicating, riveting, page-turning instruction manual on the palpable healing power of love and forgiveness. Every word in this book is as honest and courageous as any I've ever read, and I've read a lot."

— ROBIN OLIVEIRA, *NEW YORK TIMES* BESTSELLING AUTHOR OF
MY NAME IS MARY SUTTER

"*Dog Medicine* is so powerfully written, so lyrical and true, I felt I'd experienced every moment, all the loss, the crushing depression, the compassion, the great unstoppable love. So much love. Julie Barton's journey with her beautiful dog Bunker from despair to hope was a profound exercise in how to be healed. For that, I'm deeply grateful for having read this amazing book."

— ALAN HEATHCOCK, AUTHOR OF *VOLT*

"Anyone who has ever loved a dog will relate to Julie Barton's *Dog Medicine*. This memoir is a heartfelt tribute to man's best friend."

— Elliott Holt, author of *You Are One of Them*

"Julie Barton's wise, wonderful, impeccably written memoir is not just a book about how a puppy can help keep at bay the gray wolf of depression. It's also a book filled with love stories and stories of people finding their better selves, all dramatized with novelistic suspense and complexity. In this age of hour-long therapy shows and sensationalistic self-depiction, Barton's book holds true wisdom as it tells the hard-earned truths of mental illness, self-doubt, abuse, hope, family, forgiveness, connection with self and others, and finally something close to salvation. Barton gives real insight, conveyed through incisive, evocative prose. And she proves the adage that purpose comes not only from how well we are loved but by how well we love."

— Tim Parrish, author of *Fear and What Follows* and *The Jumper*

"A raw and honest memoir about Julie Barton's clinical depression and how the love of a dog helped pull her back from hell. An eloquent testament to the resilience of humans and the healing power of canine love."

— Susan Richards, *New York Times* bestselling author of
Chosen by a Horse

"It is not easy to explore the frightening landscape of depression with depth and surprising beauty. But Julie Barton has done just that. As someone who has lived with chronic depression for many years, I can tell you from personal experience how daunting and misunderstood this disease is. Not surprising that it takes the love and loyalty and unwavering sanity of a dog—any pet, really — to reach those of us struggling to find a way through the grips of melancholy. This, I know from experience, too. Read this book if you or someone you love is wrestling with depression. Read this book if you love dogs. Read this book if you want to remember what hope feels like. Just read this book."

— Susan Chernak McElroy, *New York Times* bestselling
author of *Animals as Teachers and Healers*

"Julie Barton was haunted by a major depression that threatened to topple her. What could one small puppy, Bunker, do in the face of such calamity? Only when Barton created a sacred place where she and Bunker could meet, a place without ridicule, doubt, sorrow, or anger, could the true healing begin. Her meticulous rendering of this transformation honors the power of love."

— JACQUELINE R. SHEEHAN, *NEW YORK TIMES* BESTSELLING
AUTHOR OF *LOST & FOUND*

"This absorbing memoir travels along the axis of depression and hope in beautifully crafted prose. Barton uses fresh language to provide a better understanding of the depths of depression, and introduces us to Bunker, her saving grace who throughout the book holds readers in their place."

— MARCELLE SOVIERO, EDITOR-IN-CHIEF OF *BRAIN, CHILD:
THE MAGAZINE FOR THINKING MOTHERS*

"In *Dog Medicine*, Julie Barton has the cure for the common memoir. Not only an account of the unshakable bond between dog and woman, her tale is a clear-eyed exploration of love, both given and received, which heals our damaged souls and makes us whole again. You'll come back to this book again and again."

— SAMANTHA DUNN, AUTHOR *NOT BY ACCIDENT:
RECONSTRUCTING A CARELESS LIFE*

DOG
MEDICINE

HOW MY DOG SAVED ME
FROM MYSELF

JULIE
BARTON

DOG MEDICINE © 2015 by Julie Barton. All rights reserved. No part of this book may be reproduced in any form whatsoever, by photography or xerography or by any other means, by broadcast or transmission, by translation into any kind of language, nor by recording electronically or otherwise, without permission in writing from the author, except by a reviewer, who may quote brief passages in critical articles or reviews.

The Eckhart Tolle quote is taken from the book *Guardians of Being*. Words copyright © 2009 by Eckhart Tolle. MUTTS artwork copyright © 2009 by Patrick McDonnell. Reprinted with permission of New World Library, Novato, CA. www.newworldlibrary.com.

Excerpt from WOMEN WHO RUN WITH THE WOLVES by Clarissa Pinkola Estés, Ph.D., copyright © 1992, 1995 by Clarissa Pinkola Estés, Ph.D. Used by permission of Ballantine Books, an imprint of Random House, a division of Penguin Random House LLC. All rights reserved.

ISBNs: 978-0-9863607-8-7 (paperback); 978-0-9863607-9-4 (ePub); 978-0-9863607-7-0 (Kindle)

Cover and interior design by Ryan Scheife / Mayfly Design
and typeset in the Garamond Premier Pro typeface
Author photo by Colleen Gallagher
Author with soulmate photo by Heather Knape, heatherknape.com
Cover photo by Bev Sparks, dogphotography.com

Printed in the United States of America
First Printing: 2015

19 18 17 16 15   5 4 3 2 1

Think Piece Publishing
Resiliency Stories. Health Advocacy. It's a Living Thing.

www.thinkpiecepublishing.com

*For Greg, Mom and Dad,
and forever and always, for Bunker.*

*The vital function that pets fulfill in this world
hasn't fully been recognized.*

They keep millions of people sane.

*When you pet a dog or listen to a cat purring, thinking
may subside for a moment and a space of stillness
arises within you, a doorway into Being.*

—ECKHART TOLLE

Listen with the soul-hearing now,
for that is the mission of story.

—Clarissa Pinkola Estés

PROLOGUE

I believe that when I was suffering most dearly, the universe sent me a healer in the form of a dog. Some people laugh at this idea, think it's childish, strange, or foolish. That's fine. Others nod and know exactly what I mean.

I've spent the last several years writing about my beloved Bunker. I wrote this book to share some of his wisdom because it truly was medicine to me.

Thank you for trusting me to take you on this journey. Be it a dog, a cat, a horse, any animal, really, I hope you will see yourself and your beloved pet in this story. This is my story, but I would be willing to guess, if you've picked up this book, it's a lot like your story as well.

Part I

BOILING POINT, NEW YORK CITY
APRIL 16, 1996

The walk from the subway to my apartment was six blocks, but I wasn't sure I would make it. I focused on the ground: the scuffed floor of the 4 train, the gum-strewn steps to 86th Street, the swirling black puddle at the corner of Lexington and 85th. I'd lived in Manhattan for almost a year, since one week after graduating from college in Ohio. I'd spent that year as an assistant editor at a book publisher in SoHo. My name appeared in the credits of two books. My boss called me his best assistant ever. I had scraped together enough money to pay my rent and bills, on time. I had caring friends and supportive parents who wanted me to succeed. And I was about to have a breakdown.

Only a few blocks out of the subway station, bloody thoughts descended: *Walk into the path of that cab speeding up Lexington Avenue. Step in front of that oncoming bus.* These were not voices in my head; they were rogue thoughts, terrible thoughts that I did not know how to control.

If you passed me on the street, you would have seen a tired, twenty-something woman. You'd probably think I was hung over or hadn't eaten a vegetable in months, the latter being mostly accurate. I was tall, usually wearing a baggy shirt over a long black skirt and my worn-out steel-toed Doc Martens. My hair, formerly long and blonde and flowing halfway down my back, was chopped at my ears and had faded to a brown that looked mostly gray in store-window reflections—the result of an ill-advised trip to the drugstore and a three-dollar bottle of hair dye.

I rounded the corner on 82nd Street, past the brownstones with their bay windows and heavy doors, past P.S. 290, where I rarely saw any children. I climbed the steps to my first-floor apartment, unlocked two security doors, turned three more locks, then shuffled in, finally alone. I bolted the door behind me. My apartment smelled like sour milk and dust. For a first apartment out of college, the place was fine: two small, stacked rooms connected by a steep wooden staircase. Upstairs, exposed brick stood opposite a small corner kitchen. Downstairs, they'd carved out just enough space for a small bathroom and bedroom, forever dark and damp, the windows five feet off the floor, allowing only a view of feet and legs ambling by.

The living room had no furniture, just my stereo, the one I'd had since high school. Next to it was a collapsed pile of CDs and cassettes: Van Morrison, Ani DiFranco, Tori Amos, Big Star, Ella Fitzgerald, Metallica. These were my companions in my darkest hours, this music in my ears, because in silence, I could only hear the thoughts in my head. They were thoughts that I did not notice or question, thoughts that said I was worthless, dumb, ugly, and weak. Wrong in every way. Wrong for being alive.

I began to boil water for pasta. I turned on the electric burner, filled the pot with water, and put it on the stove. Such an act might seem trivial, but I felt as if I'd just lifted a boulder. Small tasks had recently become extraordinarily difficult. Putting on shoes. Buttoning a shirt. Waking in the morning. I stood in front of the stove with my eyes closed.

Then I sat down on the floor, wooden spoon in hand. I can't say whether I was conscious of what I was doing. I remember it, if that means anything. The water began to boil. Erupting water droplets popped and sizzled on the electric burner. I blinked, flattened one palm on the dusty hardwood floor and slid down so that I was lying on the kitchen's scuffed planks. My left eyelid twitched.

I imagined myself a robot losing power, or a marionette with two snapped strings. I needed to reach the phone. I needed help. Something was really wrong. I recognized, vaguely, that the kitchen floor was an odd place to fall asleep. Then I noticed that the refrigerator door had an old brown sauce stain, a dried, stopped drip. I studied it because it didn't belong there. I didn't belong there. My head on my arm, a twitch in my spine, and I was gone.

All sounds became one enormous echo: the cars honking outside, the pigeons' flapping wings, the people walking and talking outside, the hum of the refrigerator. I lay numb, thinking, *nervous breakdown, nervous breakdown.* The words echoed in my head, a sorrowful chant, a skipping song. *You're so dramatic,* the thoughts continued. *You're not having a nervous breakdown. You're just a fuck-up. Just kill yourself. Just tie a rope around something, cinch it around your neck, and jump.*

Prior to New York City, I'd spent my entire life in Ohio, and I'd grown tired of the Midwest with its distant horizons and dark, quiet nights. Something always felt wrong. For much of high school and college, I figured that I had simply been born in the wrong place. I watched a lot of television and decided that I was a big-city girl—not an Ohio girl. It was all a simple mistake of geography. I couldn't pin my malaise on my happily married parents. My brother and I fought, badly, but that, I thought, was normal. It would take this breakdown and several years of therapy to realize that it wasn't.

My life in the city first hiccupped when an acquaintance told me that the boy I'd been dating since my junior year in college, Will, had been sleeping around while I was still at school. He was supposed to be waiting for me to join him in New York, to begin our life together. I confronted him; we fought for weeks, then broke up. He was in a band, said he needed to focus on his music. I knew it was cliché, but I suffered acutely at the demise of our romance. Will was my comfort, and now he was gone. I was a woman who couldn't feel good unless a man loved her, and it had to be this man. Will. No other. Other men scared me. I wandered alone around the city feeling as if there was no safe haven for me in the world. Then, after weeks of silence, Will would call at 3 a.m. wanting to know whether he could come over and talk. I always said yes, and I always fell back into bed with him, the longing for him so intense, I could feel it like a pull in my skin. When our relationship soured, turned emotionally unsafe, I nearly imploded.

Big-city culture shock and this difficult breakup made it clear that there was something else very wrong with me. It wasn't just that I was young, insecure, naïve, and heartbroken. It wasn't just that my boyfriend had chosen other women and his band over me. There was something dark and immovable churning inside my mind.

My roommate, Leah, had left Manhattan a few weeks prior to the day this story starts, and at the time, I was sure her swift departure was my fault. We'd met in college and roomed together in New York—not because we were great friends, but because the timing was right. She was graceful, beautiful, small, and blonde with deep-set azure eyes. She also had a boyfriend who'd graduated a year before her and lived in the city. After a few months in Manhattan, they broke up too, but she seemed fine. She went on with her life as if the breakup was his loss. When Will and I broke up, I turned lovelorn. I obsessed about his life, what he did, who he was with, which rendered me distracted and inconsistent, terrible qualities for a friend.

I woke up blinded, unable to see anything except dull gray. I put my hands in front of my face to see if my vision really was gone. My fingers barely appeared through a thick fog. I coughed hard. My lungs seemed filled with hot cotton. There was a bleak smell, like lit charcoal. I waved my arm, and the back of my knuckles hit the refrigerator. There was the drip that didn't belong.

I smelled smoke. I fumbled from the refrigerator to the stove, wheezing now. If my apartment had an operative smoke alarm, it would have been blaring. I turned off the burner and listened to the pot crackle before I lay down and fell back into the darkness.

When I awoke, the sun was shining. Cars were honking. Morning.

Home. I need to call home.

Through a still smoky haze, I became aware that I was sobbing. I'd been on the kitchen floor all night. I coughed and wheezed. My teeth clenched. The sorrow rushed in so fiercely that I imagined it might vaporize me, burst me into millions of tiny molecules. The terrible, lonely, indescribable feeling that had lingered just beneath my skin for so long had finally taken over. As I wept, the thoughts came: *You're so stupid. Get up and go to work like everyone else in the world. What makes you think you're so special that you get to lie on the floor all day?*

I woke again, no memory of falling asleep. I crawled across the floor, one elbow at a time, stopping to cry and cough, then tumble back into slumber. Sleep came as such a blessing. I was so tired.

Mid-morning, with the smoke mostly dissipated, I reached the phone. I slept with the receiver cradled on my chest and startled awake when it screeched off the hook. I pressed the button, heard a dial tone, and called my mom at work. She was a high school teacher. I rarely called her at school, but left a message with the secretary. "Please tell her it's her daughter, and it's an emergency."

I shocked awake when the phone rang.

"Mom?" I said, my voice raspy from smoke.

"Julie? What's wrong?" she said. She waited. "Julie?" she said again, already nearing panic. Her tone came as a panacea. Someone cared. Thank God someone cared.

"Something happened," I said. I choked out a loud sob. "I think I had a breakdown or something." I lay in a nearly empty apartment with tangled hair and dark-circled eyes, and weakened legs that wouldn't stand. I had a tightness in my chest. I wanted to end my life.

"I'm coming to get you," she said. "I'm getting in the car. I'll be there in nine hours. You're coming home." I let go of the phone and it skidded across the floor.

"Thank you, Mama," I whispered, and drifted back to sleep.

My mom has since told me that she walked straight into her principal's office and said, "I need to leave. It's a family emergency."

She raced home, packed a bag, and started the nine-hour drive from Columbus, Ohio, to Manhattan. Worry kept her awake until about halfway through Pennsylvania. When she nearly fell asleep at the wheel, she exited the highway and checked into a motel, slept in her clothes, and called at 7 a.m. to tell me that she would be at my apartment before noon. "You're coming home," she said, again. I wasn't about to argue.

I was twenty-two, one year out of college, full of promise yet unable to function. I have since learned to call this feeling depression, but then I had no name for it. It was a presence, a haunting, and it had taken over. It squatted on my chest, telling me to do everyone a favor and just go.

As far as we can tell, based on American Kennel Club (AKC) records and old journals, the day I gave in to the sorrow was the same spring day that Bunker Hill was born. He was a tiny golden retriever puppy, birthed on a small family farm in central Ohio. He was one of seven in the litter, not the biggest, not the runt. He entered this world inside a laundry room, on old towels that smelled like Tide and wet dog. There was a lady there, though he couldn't see or hear her, only smell her skin. Bunker entered the world helpless and nearly inert, until his mama, big, red, gentle, and dutiful, licked him clean and he took his first breath. He was healthy male number two, a furry mass of longing and need. He was blind and deaf and toothless, unable to regulate his body temperature, unable to even relieve himself without his mama's stimulation. He wasn't anything but a wiggly worm of a pup, eyes closed, ears not grown. He searched desperately for his mother, for her nourishment, her touch, her warmth and care.

Just like me.

VERY SPECIAL ME, OHIO
FALL 1982

I still have a journal that my parents gave me for my ninth birthday. It was one of the first places I looked for messages from my childhood after collapsing on the floor in New York. The journal was called *Very Special Me: A Book About Myself from Head to Toe.* The book's bright-yellow cover had a smiling unisex kid holding a paintbrush. After my last birthday party guest left, I rushed to my bedroom to begin writing my fill-in-the-blank autobiography. I snuggled in my bed and wrote that my hair was the color of *straw* and my eyes were like *brownies.* I said that my favorite color was *green.* My favorite TV shows were *Fame* and *Smurfs,* and my favorite books were *Charlotte's Web* and *The Wind in the Willows.* I wrote that on rainy days, I liked to *write and sleep.*

The book's page about feelings said, "I have a lot of different feelings..." I filled in the blanks.

I'm really happy when *my dad's happy.*

I'm really sad when *I'm alone.*

I feel mad when *my brother teases me.*

And I really feel hurt when *my brother hurts me.*

I drew a small frowning face with two teardrops coming out of each blackened eye. I wrote, "I can count to *eight* without blinking and *my dog* is beautiful and *bruises* are ugly."

By then I had a lot of bruises. They were on my arms, mostly. My brother's favorite place to hit me was on my upper arms, but I also had marks on my legs where he would kick me or toss a chair in my path. The hitting came sporadically and usually when we were alone. When my parents weren't around he'd hiss, "Loser. Look at you and your ugly face." He'd fake a punch and laugh when I flinched. Those fake punches left me nervous and jangled.

Many older brothers are mean and unhappy. I didn't think it was out of the ordinary that mine called me names: bitch, whore, loser, idiot, ugly, weirdo, fuck-face. And he hit me. Hard. He spit in my face. He pushed me down. He stepped on me. He pulled my hair. He chased me with knives. I didn't understand that Clay was struggling. I thought that this was how all older brothers behaved. I didn't know that our father's long hours at work affected him, or that our mother's emotional disconnectedness left him adrift. I just knew that he hated me, that I could do nothing right in his presence, that I was unsafe in my own home. It didn't help that I was an intensely sensitive kid. I imagined that my stuffed animals had feelings, so I read them Beatrix Potter books and then gently tucked them in bed.

Once, Clay pushed me so hard that I ricocheted against a wall and then fell headfirst into a hinge on our laundry room door. He pushed me because I asked, one too many times, which girl he and his friend thought was the prettiest in the 1983 *Sports Illustrated* Swimsuit Issue, the one with Cheryl Tiegs on the cover, leaning into a waterfall in a nearly transparent white one-piece bathing suit.

My dad heard the crash and came running from his office to find me lying unconscious in a pool of blood. I woke disoriented, my father hovering over me, yelling, panicked. He carried me to the car and raced to an emergency room where the loveliest nurse held my hand as a female doctor with a brown ponytail sewed five stitches into my head. I remember thinking that those women glowed like angels. When we got home, my father screamed at Clay behind locked doors, and I felt responsible. I shouldn't have bothered him and his friend. I wanted my father to stop yelling, because soon, I knew, Dad would go back to work and I'd be defenseless again, with an even angrier foe.

The scar has since healed into a pink crescent moon on my

right temple, the opening like a slow leak that drained me of hope, self-love, and faith. I've spent countless hours trying to sort out my sibling relationship both in therapy and in writing. I have tried to understand where my parents were during these attacks and why they weren't helping.

My father worked extraordinarily long hours as a litigator in a firm in downtown Columbus. Money always seemed tight, so his work was paramount. Our family's mood fluctuated with his stress. If he had a big trial coming up, we were not to bother him. If he lost his most recent case, we were also not to bother him. He did not have time to pay attention to what he perceived as inconsequential sibling squabbles. He grew up an only child, had no familial comparison against which to gauge his children's battles. When, as an adult, I asked him why he didn't help us, he said that he wasn't around to see much of the drama, and that he honestly did not know that our rivalry was that bad.

My mom couldn't handle us. She said that, growing up, she and her two sisters fought, but it was over things like hair curlers, and they rarely raised a hand to each other. This was new territory for her, too. Her approach to our dysfunctional relationship was to simply hope for the best. She would try to pretend that things were fine. Maybe then, she reasoned, they would be. She sometimes left the room when we started physically fighting. When I was an adult, she told me that once she hid under the bed during a particularly bad fight. She said that she'd seen on a TV talk show—maybe *Phil Donahue*—that siblings fight for their parents' attention. If the parents aren't around, they said, the kids won't fight. I can't help but picture my mother rolling under the bed as I got pummeled a few rooms away. She was trying to do the right thing.

I understood early on that my parents felt ill-equipped to deal with our rivalry, and that I was on my own. I know now that the reasons Clay hurt me are his alone. He has since apologized in a way that is both sincere and distant. He feels bad, but the fact that he doesn't recall many of the incidents between us that are seared in my memory makes me wonder if his trauma was so deep that his mind has erased his past, or worse, if I'm remembering it wrong. Which is why I still finger the crescent moon scar on my right temple. It's proof that this happened, that I was hurt. Of course, it's possible that I would've become depressed around age twenty-two even if I'd grown up with no childhood trauma. Most cases of mental illness start in the late teen years and culminate in the early twenties, so I was right on time.

The moon on the day of my birth, October 1, 1973, was a crescent moon, waxing, its bulbous surface 24 percent visible from earth, the exact shape and size of the scar on my temple. This is how I am certain that this sibling trauma is part of my story to tell. But these stories push and pull at me and leave me mercurial and conflicted. One minute I feel deep empathy for my brother, who must have been hurting terribly. The next minute I am furious: deep-down, want-to-smash-something enraged. Why did no one help me?

Of course, I didn't yet understand, when I was lying on the floor in Manhattan, how any of this had affected me. I simply thought that I was weak and stupid. As I broke down on that kitchen floor, I was divorced from my brain—just a pinging signal in there— bouncing back and forth between expectation and demand, not at all connected to the little girl buried under all that dark and heavy moon dust.

Quarter Eclipse, New York City
April 17, 1996

I woke disoriented. My head pounded. It took me several seconds to realize that the phone was ringing. I crawled to it and pushed the answer button. "Hello?"

"Hi, honey," my mother said, her voice its usual singsong. "I'm just east of Harrisburg, Pennsylvania. I'm fueling up and I'll be there by noon."

"Okay," I said, my voice hoarse.

"I'll see you really soon," she said. "Start packing. You're coming home."

I heard the phone disconnect. I wanted to ask her what time it was. Morning? Night?

I woke again. This kind of falling asleep was like fainting. There was no warning; here one minute, gone the next with no inkling of how long I'd been away. Waking up proved a perpetual disorientation, but now I had to pee. I sat up slowly. The room spun. This room, that I'd planned to use as my living room after Leah left, held nothing but a dresser that I'd salvaged from the street and a phone base dangling from a kinked wire. The singed pan squatted on the tiny stove; the ripped-open pasta box littered the counter.

Sitting up made me see stars and blue spots. I sat, legs straight out, hands limp, until the roaring in my ears stopped. My skin squeaked on the floor. I pushed myself up, ass high in the air, wobbly, like a drunkard. I leaned, winded, against the brick wall. The thoughts in my head that I did not yet recognize said: *You are stupid and weak. You are fat and ugly and you can't handle anything.*

This whole apartment can't wait for you to take your terrible energy and go. Thoughts become beliefs—and I believed I was worthless. I believed that inanimate spaces hated me. These thoughts were as normal to me as hunger pangs or fatigue, simply part of my being.

Eventually I made it down the stairs into the shower with one urgent thought: My mom would be knocking on the door in a few hours. I didn't want her to see how bad it really was.

In the shower, the water on my face felt like an angel's hands. I was so grateful for the touch that I began to weep. Then the crying became strange: jagged and shrieking. Because what kind of person imagines that water is an angel running her fingers through her hair? I knew what kind of person imagined that—an insane person. A person bound for life with a garbage bag coat, urine-soaked pants, and a shopping cart for a bank account.

Somewhere in the back of my mind, I saw the me that was really *me*, the little orb of untouched soul deep in there, and she was giving up. All I heard from inside the water was, "Let go. Just let go. It's too hard. It's time to let go."

So I began to do exactly that. I sat on the floor of the shower and howled. I didn't know what was wrong with me. I'd lost my boyfriend, yes. I was bored at my job, yes. My friends were sick of my malaise, yes. But those problems did not warrant this kind of agony. I began to contemplate the relief of ending my life.

For years I had worked to build an emotional dam to fend off the sorrow. But somehow, after college, it was as if a bigger crack in my temple had developed. The moon was waxing. I hated to be looked at. Riding the subway to work every day was torturous because of all the eyes. So many eyes. The terrible thoughts in my head convinced me that everyone looked at me with disgust.

The door's buzzer woke me. I had once again fallen into sleep like an untethered astronaut drifting into space. I shivered, failing to stay warm under my scratchy old bath towel with the blue and red sailboats. The buzzer squawked again, relentless. I sat up, my naked body heavy, and climbed the stairs clutching the damp towel to my chest. The buzzer blared and I wanted to yell that I was coming, but I didn't have enough air or energy or will.

I pushed the button to unlock the building's front door. Then I undid all four locks, my eyes barely opened. I knew that this moment was a turning point. When I let my mother in, I was going to give up and go back to Ohio. I would leave behind any hope of reuniting with Will, the man I thought I needed. I would give up on life in New York. I might even give up on living.

On April 17, 1996, the second day of Bunker's life and my second day on the floor, there was a partial solar eclipse. The moon passed between the sun and the earth, obscuring the light. Though only visible from the deepest reaches of the southern hemisphere, the moon, always my ally, was blocking the sun, allowing for darkness.

No light for me. No light for Bunker, whose eyes were not yet open. Like round pegs sliding into round holes, darkness was our meeting place, our psychic gathering spot. We didn't know it, but we were, at the dark moment when the moon slid over the sun, beginning the long and difficult rest that would precede our union, and the light.

Suburban Graffiti, Ohio

1983

I was ten, my brother thirteen, and we were fighting again. He chased me down the hallway to my bedroom. I leapt into my bedroom, breathless. There was just enough time to slam the door and lock it. I climbed on my bed and scooted back into the corner as he reached my door and began pounding. He kicked it and it wobbled, echoing with a strange, hollow sound—like a slide guitar. He punched the door and it rattled so hard that the wall behind my head shook.

"Open the fucking door!" he screamed. I pulled my knees to my chest, pressed my back into the corner, and watched my door shiver under the weight of his force. I don't remember why he was so mad. My mom was home but outside raking leaves. My dad was at work.

With each hit or kick, Clay yelled obscenities like "Fucking bitch! I'm going to fucking rip your *head* off!" I saw the top left panel of the door splinter first, and then the whole thing came off its hinges. The door split from the doorjamb and drifted inward, landing with a barely perceptible thud onto my lime-green carpet. A tree falling in the forest. He lunged at me on my white wicker bed with the eyelet sheets, punching my arms, pinning me down, and adjusting his fist so his middle knuckle stuck out as he punched the same spot over and over again. I slid down, my head pressed so hard against the flowered wallpaper that one ear began to ring. My hair snagged on the wicker headboard.

I couldn't push him away. He was over six feet tall at thirteen years old, and overweight. "Get off me!" I screamed and pushed, but my strength was one-third of his.

He spat in my eyes before standing up. "You're lucky I didn't kill you," he said. "Because I could, you know." I sat up on my bed, trying to look defiant, patting down my tangled hair. He faked another punch that landed inches from my face. I flinched, my hands pushing out into the air, reaching nothing. When I opened my eyes, he was walking away.

I don't know where Clay went after the fight. Maybe he was hiding because my fallen bedroom door was proof of his rage. I tip-toed past his bedroom then sprinted down the long hallway to my parents' room. "Mom!" I screamed, as soon as I heard the swish of a drawer opening in her bedroom. "Clay broke my door! My whole entire door! He knocked it down!"

She was peeling off dirty gardening clothes. Each autumn, she spent entire weekends raking up every fallen leaf on our three acres. She had a thin film of sweat on her face. Flecks of dirt and leaves clung to her skin and hair. "Just stay away from him," she sighed. She took a towel and held it to her face, pulling in a deep breath. My mother hated our fighting. She didn't understand it and couldn't make us stop.

I didn't say anything else. I sat on her bed while she undressed in silence and stepped into her bathroom's powder-blue-tiled shower. I borrowed a nail clipper from my dad's nightstand and began trimming my toenails, careful not to leave the cuttings on their flowered comforter.

Later, when Clay left for a friend's house and it was safe to return to my bedroom, I found my door still lying on the carpet like a fallen soldier that had tried but failed to protect me. As I maneuvered to step over the split open wood, something caught my eye. Jagged graffiti was scrawled on my doorjamb: "Loser," "Lesbian," "Whore," and "Everyone Hates You." I gasped. I was upset that he'd written these words, but more terrified that someone might see them. Because what Clay thought about me, I thought about myself. He was older, stronger, smarter. I had no proof of anything else, and I feared that my parents and friends would see the graffiti and agree with him. I grabbed an eraser from my desk but couldn't rub away the words. Clay had written in pen and with such pressure that the letters were carved into the wood.

Partial Eclipse, New York City
April 17, 1996

My mom stood in my doorway, and the sight of her was the only thing that made sense: her light-blue eyes, her small, industrious hands, her smell so familiar, like coffee, bed sheets, and perfume. She hugged me, squeezed tight, but I was too weak to return the gesture. "How are you?" she said, holding me at the small of my back. "Are you feeling okay?"

"I need to lie down," I said, turning away. I limped down the stairs to the bed. She put her purse on the floor and followed me.

"Can you tell me what happened?" she said, sitting on the edge of my mattress.

"Not really." I got under the covers, still wearing only a towel. The overhead lights hurt my eyes so I kept them closed. "I'm just so, so tired."

I was tired, but also terrified. I knew that something had happened, but all I could think about was that I did not know what I was going to do with my life. I'd be back in Ohio, in my parents' house, with no job, no boyfriend, no prospects, no friends, no future.

"Okay, honey," she said. "You sleep."

"Okay," I said, noting a whisper of relief that I wasn't alone before falling into the fainting sleep.

When I awoke, my apartment smelled like coffee, something I didn't drink. I squinted and saw my mom trying to sponge-clean my bathroom as quietly as possible. When I shifted, she put down the coffee and cleaning supplies and came to me. She sat on the mattress's edge, like she had so many times when I was a child, and she pushed the hair away from my face, behind my ear. With that small gesture, my chin quivered and tears came.

"You've been asleep for three hours," she said. "I've already started packing your things. You need to go tell your boss you're leaving." She gave me a smile and then turned back to work on the bathroom.

My mom is *always* smiling. She's only five feet, four inches tall but truly capable of pretty much any physical task. I've seen her rip out entire bushes with four-foot deep roots using only her pink-garden-gloved hands. I've seen her hack a snake in half with a hoe. I've watched her, for years, mow her own multi-acre lawn with a John Deere tractor mower—her long hair pushed inside a baseball cap. She's not afraid to get dirt under her fingernails, but she also likes to put on a dress and go to a party. Her brown hair has always been long, at least a few inches past her shoulders. She's got periwinkle-blue eyes and was the college homecoming queen at the football game at which my father caught the winning touchdown. She wears perfume almost daily, Estée Lauder's Knowing. That smell, to me, is unconditional love. And even though things were moving fast, I knew that if I followed her simple directions, she would take care of me. Things might even be okay.

The thing was, this was 1996. Mental illness wasn't much talked about then. My parents had no idea what major clinical depression was, nor did I. Bad days? Sure. In a rough patch? Of course. But something medically wrong? We were going to have to find our way to that diagnosis by letting the blackness come way, way too close to our doorstep.

With my mother's help, I managed to get up and get dressed. I took a cab to SoHo to tell my boss I was quitting. I felt like I was walking on rubber bands, but I made it. It was 3 p.m. when I wandered quietly into the office after missing a day and a half of work. My boss greeted me with a glance that read "Where on earth have you been?" I tried to calmly explain that I was quitting, but instead

I burst into hysterical sobs saying, "Something's happened. I need to leave. I have to go. I'm leaving New York."

He had no idea what to say except, "Okay. Calm down." I left ten minutes later after a cursory explanation of my desk and files, apologizing through tears.

I rode the subway back uptown. I took the train because hailing a cab seemed too difficult a task. Again, I imagined that every subway passenger found my flaws repulsive: my pimples, my damaged hair and tear-streaked cheeks. Except this time, I decided to look up. I took an inventory of these people, knowing that I would not ride the subway again for a very long time. Everyone was frowning. Connection, that thing I was longing for so desperately, was forbidden in Manhattan's underground. It was as if we were all different ions bouncing around, too negatively charged to connect in any way. Long ago, my mind had turned the anonymity and disconnection of the subway inward. The thoughts chimed in: *Why would anyone want to look at you anyway? You're awful and stupid and your face is hideous.*

The train screeched to a stop at 86th Street and I slid sideways through the barely opened doors. I kept my head down and walked back to my apartment wishing I could fall into the concrete and melt away. My thoughts veered dark again: *Just step out into the street into the path of that yellow cab. It'll be so easy. You'll be knocked out and won't feel anything.* But I knew my mom was waiting for me.

When I rounded the corner onto 82nd Street, I saw that she had packed my entire apartment and somehow managed to drag my crappy furniture out to the sidewalk for passersby to take. Leave it to my small but formidable mother to figure out a way to pack an entire apartment, including a bunny in a cage, into a car in one short afternoon. I walked inside and there was nothing left, just a few dust balls, wires, and the burnt pot in the kitchen. I wanted to sit down on that floor and weep. But my mom grabbed my hand, twisted the doorknob so it would lock, tossed the keys on the floor, and heaved the door shut.

We walked down the steps to her car, double-parked and already running. "Hop in," she said, holding me by my waist. "We'll be home soon."

I climbed into her car in slow motion. She reclined the passenger seat of the SUV and buckled me in as I cried. She didn't ask what was wrong. She just pushed my hair behind my ear in the way that made me feel like a child again, safe in bed with the trees and deer and moon outside my room to protect me. Tears dripped into my ears and down my neck as we drove out of Manhattan. I was asleep before we left the city.

Here's part of why my road to despair is confusing: most of the time, my parents showed up. If I had a crisis at school, my dad would drop his papers, leave work, and race to find me. That happened once in high school after I failed a French exam. After I called him in tears, my dad sped to my school, picked me up, and took me out for doughnuts and chocolate milk, reminding me that my grade on a dumb French test would not dictate my future. And when I was seventeen, after I lost my virginity and was convinced I was pregnant, my mom took me to the drugstore to buy the right kind of test after the cheaper test I'd bought yielded a positive result. Throughout the whole ordeal, she was calm, kind, and understanding. I remember her holding my hand.

These were, by many measures, phenomenal parents. So why hadn't they helped when it came to the violent fights between their children? I still don't know the answer to this question. I have many theories, but the fact is that even the most wonderful, caring, kind, well-meaning parents can make mistakes. Theirs was a mistake of inattention. It was a crime of omission. I guess they just didn't know how.

At four days old, a puppy is still in complete darkness. His eyes haven't opened, his range of movement is small, his only goal warmth and food. He fights his siblings to get to his mother's belly and then follows his nose to an unoccupied teat. When he finds it, he pulls with all his might, yanking and clawing in an effort to stimulate milk. His mama's nipples are reddened, stretched to ten times their normal size, swollen, and full. But she knows that her puppies need her. They need endless love and care from their mother, and they bark and bite and scratch her until they exhaust themselves. Of course the mother tolerates almost all of it. She'll lie with her eyes closed, her vulnerable abdomen exposed, breathing fast and hard but keeping perfectly still so her fragile little babies can get what they need to grow up and survive in the world. Much of it is instinct; the rest is pure love.

Waning Magic, Ohio
1984

As a child, I talked to trees. I had a best-friend tree, a century-old beech that I'd named "Alice." If you'd asked me when I was eight, I would've told you that Alice was like my great-grandma. She loved me most of all. She wanted me to visit every day. She talked to me kindly. She left me presents: five happy ladybugs, a monarch circling her trunk. She told me not to worry, that everything would be okay.

I spent whole days wandering alone through the farmland near our house. I'd pack a peanut butter and jelly sandwich in a paper bag, then cut through the Killians' yard across the street and slip under the stretched-out barbed-wire fence. Once I got under that fence, there was nothing but cornfields, forests, farmland, and safety.

Just past the first cornfield to the right, tucked away as if forgotten, sat Lehman's Pond, a tiny body of water brimming with wildlife: frogs, fish, snakes, birds, snails, bugs. There was an old abandoned barn there, or maybe it was a field worker's house. It sat nearly over the pond, stood two stories tall, though one whole wall had fallen off exposing the rotting stairway and flimsy construction. Parts of the wood were still painted red and white. I could sit in the barn with my feet dangling off the rotting floor and my toes would touch the pond's water. For hours I would read, nap, skip rocks, or catch frogs.

Next to Lehman's Pond lived a grove of tall pine trees planted in four rows. Those trees, at least fifty years old, created this magical outdoor room with branches for a ceiling and a pine needle carpet that muted all the sounds of the forest. If I sat there long enough, quiet enough, I could hear nothing—and everything. I could hear a bird landing on a branch. I could hear a leaf fall to the ground. A hummingbird passing through sounded like the turn of a speeding bicycle wheel.

Once, after sitting for some time, I heard the hoof-fall crackle of a mama deer wandering through with her fawn. When she noticed me, she froze, a dark black eye sparkling. She led her fawn around me, not ten feet from my scabby knees, toward the pond for a sip of water. Her fawn's legs were impossibly thin, the white spots on his back still prominent. His little tail flitted to attention. His hooves were barely the size of a tube of Chapstick. He watched me warily as he crossed the pine grove. Then, in the clearing, he stopped. We locked eyes for what seemed like an eternity. Something passed between us. Something that I decided was magical. I believed then that I could talk to him. He understood me. Animals understood me. The thought was enormously comforting. I had an ally. The fawn turned and caught up with his mama, and they jumped into the rows of corn and out of sight.

I wasn't yet ten years old, and I felt so connected to the land, to the trees, to the animals passing by. I considered myself one of them—part of nature's tribe, the people of the woods, the birds, the frogs, the moon, the deer, the owls, our family dog. They were my companions, my reliable source of solace.

In the winter, there was no one to play with on quiet weekends but Alice. When it was too cold to go out and be with her, I worried. One particularly frigid winter afternoon, I watched Alice swaying in the icy blast of a snowstorm. I imagined what it would be like to have my fingers exposed, fifty feet high, all winter long. Such an existence would be too awful; I needed to do something.

I pulled two of my baby blankets out of my closet and went to the garage and pulled on my snow boots. Outside I had to blink to keep my eyelashes from sticking with freeze. I struggled with the blankets but managed to snag the fabric on her bark and walk around her trunk. I tied two corners of the blankets together then safety-pinned the other side. She looked like she was wearing a too-small apron, but I wrapped my arms around her anyway. "I hope this helps, Alice," I whispered. "Spring will come soon." I patted her and ran back inside.

For days, I paused in the dining room, watching her from inside the house, her blankets soon crusted with ice. While I huddled under several layers of blankets at night, I feared that the sound of the wind or the crackling of branches was the beginning of Alice's demise. If she fell, she wouldn't crush our house, but the tips of her branches might graze the windows, as if to try to grasp us, to ask us to save her, even though she knew there was nothing we could do as she fell to her death.

Men, Kenyon College & New York City
Winters 1994 and 1995

If my conflicted relationship with my brother cracked the foundation of my self-worth, my New York boyfriend, Will, was the final invasion of termites that left the whole structure condemned. I met him at an apartment party when I was a junior in college. He was a senior with a goatee and a long brown ponytail: not my type at all. I was into extra-handsome bad boys, rugged-looking men who didn't talk much and would take me home and have their way with me. Aloof men were good. Men who blew off their girlfriends for fraternity brothers were no problem for me. Men who wanted sex and lots of it but then ignored me in the cafeteria were fine. Men were men; I expected desertion and mistreatment.

At this party, Will sat next to me as a group of about six of us played poker. His voice was sexy, deep, and resounding, but I wasn't into the sensitive ponytail look. Which is why it was odd when I leaned my elbow on his leg to grab a card from the table and felt an electric connection. We looked at each other; we'd both felt the jolt.

A few days later I ran into Will at the bookstore. I didn't recognize him in the sobering light of day. He was skinny, six feet tall, and probably weighed less than me. His pants practically fell off when he stood up to say hello.

"Hey, Julie. I've been looking for you. Want to go to the Philander's Phling with me?"

I laughed, sure he was joking. Who invites a girl to a dance in college? The look on his face told me this was no joke, and I was an asshole.

"Oh!" I said. "Uh, okay."

"Great," he said. "I'll meet you outside of Peirce Hall at 9 p.m. sharp. Saturday. Okay?"

"Okay," I said, walking away. I waved, cursing myself for not thinking of a quick excuse.

Philander Chase was the founder of Kenyon College. His namesake party was an annual dance held in an effort to beat the February (Phebruary) blahs. Dorks and dweebs made plans to go to Philander's Phling. Cool kids showed up half wasted and underdressed. I wanted to identify in the latter camp, but I couldn't be rude. So I put on an old strapless black dress with a ruffle around the knee that I'd worn to countless dances in high school and showed up at 9 p.m., shivering in high heels and pantyhose in the dark of an Ohio winter night.

My friends thought it was good that I was branching out. They were tired of me pining for my ex-boyfriend, Brian, the boy I'd dated from the first month of my freshman year on and off through my junior year. I loved him in that first-love kind of way, the desperate, once-in-a-lifetime bliss of falling for someone for the very first time. But as far as my friends were concerned, Brian had treated me with such disrespect that they could not make sense of why I would pine for him. Our relationship was passionate and dysfunctional. We exchanged handwritten letters with tearstains blurring the words. He was a beautiful boy: hazel eyes with curly dark hair, a state champion swimmer, six foot two with shoulders twice as wide as mine. His legs were long and lean, and his attention to me was inconsistent and intoxicating. There were cheating scandals both during our relationship and after we'd broken up. We'd see each other at a party and fall into bed again, just for a night. I'd pray that in the morning he would confess his undying love, say our breakup was the biggest regret of his life. But in the harsh light of day, he'd say, "You should probably just go."

I couldn't get enough of Brian's bad-love adrenaline, and at the time I didn't question why. Not only did I not question unhealthy love, I sought it out. I wasn't about to turn around and start dating Will, the sensitive, guitar-playing ponytail guy.

I still have a picture of Will and me that night at Philander's Phling. There was a photographer walking around the dance taking pictures of each couple. In ours, Will is standing behind me, his arms around my waist. We look as if we're mid-step, leaning into the camera. My first thought when I saw the picture was that my face looked fat. But my second reaction was that I looked happy—genuinely, no fuss, happy.

After the dance we went back to my dorm room. I turned on my Tori Amos CD and on came that song that goes, "God, sometimes you just don't come through. Do you need a woman to look after you?" He held my waist firmly, pressing his hips into mine, then he slowly leaned into me. Something happened when our lips touched. It was like white light. A thunderclap. I remember thinking that this must be what they mean when they say a first kiss can be like fireworks. That was it. I was a goner.

We started spending every spare moment together. We'd make out and talk, and do everything but have sex. I told myself that I would not embark upon another dysfunctional sex-driven relationship. As if I were protecting something sacred, and finally trying to treat myself well, I decided to send him home just about every night at 2 or 3 a.m. I liked having him in my room, but I also liked when he was gone. This kind of romance felt healthy.

He played guitar and would come over to my dorm room plucking melodies while we talked about our families and childhoods. He told me he'd never met anyone like me. He said he felt safe around me. It had never occurred to me that men could feel unsafe. The men in my life never seemed to be in need of protection. His vulnerability struck me as enlightened and beautiful and rare.

Will was also the first man to make an effort to understand me sexually. He identified the massive mental hurdles between me and orgasm. He worked and worked until he could satisfy me. I told my girlfriends about him, said that I'd never had more orgasms with a man. They listened, mouths agape as I told them that he whispered crazy things to me in my dorm room late at night. "You are beautiful. I love you. I want you to come for me. Now I want you to come again." It was an epic, best-sex-ever love affair that I wanted to continue in Manhattan. We were two wounded birds who would take flight together. Our romance quickly became us against the world. We decided that just about everyone else was stupid and mean and unenlightened. The only way for us to survive would be to stick together.

When he graduated one year before me, I bought a special dress for his graduation and posed in all the pictures with him in his cap and gown. We stayed up half the night before he left for Manhattan and talked about how, while I completed my senior year, he would spend the time preparing the city for us, getting ready for our lives together there. I imagined us going to concerts: Wilco and Paul Weller and all the unsigned singer-songwriters down at the Ludlow Street Bar & Grill. I wanted to help his band book gigs, move equipment, gather fans. I would be the one in front starting the mosh pit and then stepping aside as the crowd got wild. I imagined going out drinking with our friends and sneaking away to make out with Will in dark corners before racing home to one of our apartments for loud, urgent, wildly satisfying sex. I imagined us meandering tree-lined streets in the morning, lounging on a blanket in Central Park, eating hot bagels, rehydrating with enormous bottles of water, our limbs intertwined, getting each other off under makeshift picnic blankets because the worst fate ever would be for us to be forced to keep our hands off of each other.

But within mere hours of my arrival in New York, I sensed a distance. I planned to stay with Will and his roommate in their tiny Hell's Kitchen apartment for a few weeks while Leah and I looked for our own place. I envisioned Will, me, and his roommate, Jeff, having pizza on the floor of their barely furnished apartment, Jeff thankful for a female touch. Instead Jeff asked me, "You're going to be here how long?" before ignoring me in protest, sighing heavily when he was forced to maneuver through the narrow hallway past my stuff. Will apologized to him, said, "Wasn't my idea. Fucking sucks." I felt a betrayal that was softened by my general understanding of men—that men don't like women unless women do things for them.

So one day while Will was at work, I trudged a few blocks carrying two enormous bags of his dirty laundry and, like a new and dutiful wife, laundered all of his clothes. It wasn't until I hauled the bags back to his apartment that I realized some of the clothes were still mildly damp. I folded them anyway, and when he came home from work to several neat piles of clean clothes on his bed, he didn't smile. He asked me why I'd done it. And he flatly told me that he didn't think of me as the kind of woman who would do chores for her man. I wasn't, of course, that kind of woman. I was worse: weak and terrified, a suburban girl dropped in the big city, not an ounce of self-confidence to her name. I apologized, saying something like, "Sorry. Just trying to help. Make up for crashing at your guys' place."

"Whatever," he replied, kissing the top of my head. "No big deal." When he went to his bed, he touched one of the piles and looked at me, eyes tight. "You know these are still kind of wet, right?"

"Shit," I said. I did know. I just didn't want him to notice. I don't know what I wanted. I wanted him to be gentle with me, the way he was in Ohio. New York seemed to have hardened him and weakened me. I wanted to cry and apologize and ask for his forgiveness, even though I had no idea what I needed forgiveness for. I felt adrift without his approval, his love.

A few weeks and many arguments later, I found out through a woman named Jane that Will had been cheating on me. Jane worked as the receptionist for my roommate Leah's publishing house. She was a pretty, perky brunette who always wore bright-red lipstick. We started chatting one afternoon before she knew I was Will's girlfriend. Turns out she was dating the lead singer in Will's band. Will had excluded me from all band activities, so we hadn't met yet. Jane was laughing about how all the guys in her boyfriend's band were sluts.

"Oh, yeah?" I asked. "Those guys mess around a lot?"

"Oh, my gawd," she said, her Staten Island accent curling the end of every word. "You have no idea."

"Really?"

"Oh, Jesus," she said. "The guitar player? Will? Won't leave me and my friends alone. He asks me all the time, 'Hook me up with a hot blonde.' Once," she paused and put her hand up in a way that suggested I needed to prepare myself, "I walked into Jon's apartment and saw Will *naked*, running back into Jon's bedroom where some skank was laughing and waiting for him. By the way, he apparently has a girlfriend who lives in like Idaho or something. *And* he has a nonexistent flat ass."

She was right. He had no ass.

I wandered away mid-conversation. I only remember my stomach doing that awful acidic drop. I took the elevator down and walked out into the street, headed up to Tower Records and it was there that I began to cry. I leaned on the window, my clammy forehead resting on a ten-foot-tall poster of Tupac. How could I be such a fool? How could Will do this? It was supposed to be us against the world.

I confronted Will. Initially, he weakly denied any infidelity. Then he defended himself fiercely, calling me crazy and overly sensitive, calling Jane a liar. Soon, we were fighting terribly about the truth of these rumors, about the truth of everything that had ever gone on between us. We would break up, then reunite, and break up again. Sometimes when I was with him, I found myself clearly thinking, "I don't want to be with this man." This should've meant that I could walk away. But nothing surpassed my need for Will's approval. Nothing. It was a desperate grab, something I did not know how to control.

I remember several dramatic, sob-strewn scenes in restaurants, on sidewalks, and in our respective apartments. Once, a bartender asked us to go outside because we were fighting so loudly that we were disturbing other patrons. I pined for months, unable to think of much else. I looked for him everywhere, and the fact that I pretty much never had a chance of accidentally running into him in Manhattan left me feeling stranded, alone on an island of millions.

Then he would show up at my doorstep at 3 a.m., like a miracle, several beers in, and we'd fall into each other's arms. We'd have sex, wonder aloud why we were not together, and pledge our undying love. Then in the morning the flaws would re-emerge, the hurts resurface, the arguments rewind, and we'd call it all off again. I'd be crushed. Devastated. Imagining suicide off the roof of my building. Too torn apart, I knew, for my sorrow to be just about the demise of our romance.

Total Eclipse, Pennsylvania and Ohio

April 17 and 18, 1996

My mom and I barreled through eastern Pennsylvania. We pulled into a rest stop near Allentown where, as if scripted in a stupid movie, there stood Will. He was on tour with his band, a tour funded by the bass player's dad.

"Oh, my god," I whispered to myself when our eyes locked outside the vending machines. He walked over to me and pulled me to him, pressed his whole body into mine. My mom saw us and said nothing, just walked back to the car.

"I left New York," I said into his collar. He smelled like cigarettes and beer.

"Okay," he said.

"I'm sorry," I said.

"Shhh," he pulled me close again. I still loved him. I loved his body. I loved how slight and strong it was. I had wanted to hold that body every morning and night for the rest of my life. But soon the cigarette smell became unbearable, and my mom was waiting for me. "I love you. I'll always love you," he said. I wiped my tears on my sleeve and pushed him away. His bandmates smirked as they ambled past us.

"Me too," I said. I walked to my mom's car. She sat clutching the steering wheel with the engine already running. I'd barely closed the door when she floored it and pulled away.

"You okay?" she asked, as she sped back onto the freeway, looking over her shoulder into her blind spot. "Of all the luck. I can't *believe* we ran into him here."

"Yeah," I said, buckling myself slowly. "Just drive." I closed my eyes and prepared to return to sleep. I couldn't look back.

My mom and I didn't talk for several hundred miles. I slept, then woke and sat with my head turned away from her, my nose an inch from the window until I fell asleep again. We stopped an hour or so later and spent the night in a roadside motel.

I woke in the motel, disoriented after a vivid dream of New York and Will and the life I'd abandoned. My mom tapped my shoulder, saying that it was checkout time, almost noon. "It seemed like you desperately needed some real rest." I imagined her watching me sleep, monitoring my breathing as if I were a newborn in a crib.

"Okay," I said. I stumbled to the bathroom, peed with my eyes closed, brushed my teeth, and followed her to the car. I curled up against the car window, my eyes pulling closed again, sleep taking me away.

"Only about an hour left," I heard my mom say. I opened my eyes to see my mom's small hands clutching the steering wheel, her rounded nails painted cantaloupe orange. I didn't respond, hardly awake, noting the descending sun. Leaving Manhattan felt like flipping over a topographical map. On this side, everything lay flat, concave even. After several months of tight spaces, walls, and corners, the openness of eastern Ohio was alarming.

Farmland rushed by: soybean fields, cornfields, enormous old barns. Soon the landmarks became familiar. Outside Pataskala, the tall red barn that leaned one degree short of tumbling over. Roush Hardware at the edge of town, the place Dad always bought us a cellophane-wrapped chocolate coconut haystack as a reward for tolerating his lengthy trips to the garden section. Noah's Ark Pet Store where I sold my baby hamsters and guinea pigs for twenty-nine cents each. The ice cream shop our family would drive to on a hot Sunday afternoon—rocky road for everyone but Mom, who usually just had water. Then Dublin Middle School, where Mr. Niemie, my sixth-grade English teacher, with auburn curls,

John Lennon glasses, and bright eyes, was the first teacher to tell me I should keep writing.

We turned left down Route 745 and there was Oscar's Deli, the restaurant where I had my first job as a waitress, eating more than I served, trying not to cry when the woman who wanted her eggs poached *this* way, not *that* way, sent her unsatisfactory breakfast back to the kitchen six times. Down the long road that hugged the muddy river, past mean Robbie Thompson's house, who sometimes joined Clay in his attacks, then my childhood playmate Tricia's place. I imagined that all those kids had left home and not come back. I imagined them off in medical school, law school, landing fantastic jobs, slow-dancing with lovers on sparkling rooftops.

After a few miles, we turned onto Birchwood Road, our road. We pulled up the long, slow hill that I'd jogged countless times, past Mrs. Pethel's house and Mrs. Jacoby's place, two elderly women who, on long, lonely summer days, took me in and gave me pie. Past the opening in the yard across the street that led to Lehman's Pond and the pine grove I spent countless hours wandering.

We stopped at the end of the long driveway. Mom jumped out, ran across the road to check for mail, and there was the familiar creak of the mailbox door, the echo of its closing. Then my house at dusk. Its tall central eave and big angular points modeled after Frank Lloyd Wright's designs with loads of blond wood and enormous floor-to-ceiling windows. My parents' bedroom was in the south wing, my brother's and mine in the north. In between us soared vaulted ceilings over the kitchen and living and dining rooms.

At the end of the driveway, Mom got back into the car and closed the door hard. "Ahh," she sighed. "We're home. Here we go." She eased up the long driveway. I squinted, one eye closed, blinded a bit by the waning sunlight glaring through the trees. The shafts of light made our house look like a church, a place I could come to rest my battered spirit, or a place I could come to die.

Many things can go wrong in the first few weeks of a puppy's life. He could miss out on essential care from his mother and die of malnutrition or hypothermia. His mother could develop mastitis and slowly poison him and all his littermates with the toxins in her milk. He could get crushed under the weight of his exhausted, milk-filled mama. Or there could simply be not enough milk to go around, and he'd die of hunger.

I was as raw as I'd ever been, perfectly willing to become increasingly self-destructive until I finally ended my life. My mind was not well, and I knew it, which was terrifying. Knowing that you are not rational, that your thoughts are out of control, is disorienting. It's like sitting down on a couch and then watching your body walk away without you. This is the time to ask for help. But I wasn't aware enough to know that help was what I needed. I was like a newborn too: helpless, blind, weak.

The closer I got to Ohio, the stronger the connection between me and Bunker must have become. I remember pulling into the garage thinking about the dogs of my youth, how they provided me with such solace. It occurred to me then that maybe I could try again and get my own dog. A dog I could protect. A dog that would protect me. It was just a thought.

MIDNIGHT, OHIO

1977 AND 1980

The first dog I remember loving was named Midnight. We found her abandoned in a car wash during a blizzard when I was four and my brother was seven. Family legend has her shivering in the corner with icicles dangling from her matted fur. My mom snatched her up, drove her home, and never posted "dog found" signs, because whoever owned the dog, she reasoned, was irresponsible. And besides, we all fell in love with her. My parents decided she was a cock-a-poo, half cocker spaniel and half poodle. She had soft, tight curled fur and a long, thin tail.

My dad, in particular, adored Midnight. She didn't soil the house. She didn't shed. She liked to snuggle and was interminably happy. "Midnight is the best dog we've ever had," he would say. He liked to declare a lot of wonderful things, and I loved this about him. "We are the luckiest people that she came to us. It was meant to be—for us to find her. Amazing dog, that dog." I would listen, near rapture. I felt the same way, and his similarly deep connection with our dog left me elated. Midnight would twirl adoringly at his feet and he would bend over, all six athletic feet of him, and pick her up, letting her cover his face in kisses. He'd say things like, "Oh, yes, I love you too. I love you too, good girl."

All little girls love their dogs, but I felt a desperate kind of love for Midnight. I would call her to me, and as if she knew how much I needed her, she came running. When she curled up in my lap, I felt my breathing regulate, my skin relax, my shoulders loosen. I was protective of her because our house felt safe when Midnight was around.

When Clay and I fought, Midnight hid. She would run to my parents' room, flatten her body, her back legs stretched into a frog-like splay and scoot under their bed. Then she'd army-crawl all the way to the wall, shivering. Sometimes, after the fight, I would try to coax her out, but she would look at me suspiciously from the dark corner, unmoving. Other times when she hid, I would just sit silently next to my parents' bed, waiting. Usually, she'd come out cowering, her pressed-down tail still wagging at the very tip. She would whimper a little, curl into my lap, and lick me furiously.

"It's okay," I would whisper. "We're okay." And I would tell her that sometimes people fight. Sometimes I'd cry and say I was stupid. Sometimes I'd cry and say that Clay was stupid. Most often I'd just be silent. My brother and I fought daily. We'd insult each other, yell at each other, and inevitably, he would lunge at me and hit me, hard. At seven years old, I knew what a punch to the head felt like. I knew what a kick on the shin felt like. I knew what a bad blow to the gut felt like.

One day my mom locked Midnight in the laundry closet. She said not to open the door because Midnight would bite. She held up her hand, which bore a gory brown and purple bruise.

"Midnight did that?" I asked.

"We think she hurt her back. She's really sick, honey. It hurts her to move."

"Why isn't she at the doctor?" I asked.

"I tried to take her, but she bit me when I approached her. So I called, and the vet said to just isolate her and see if she improves."

The laundry closet opened from both sides. My mom had moved the laundry basket out and lined the floor with sheets and towels. I peeked inside from a small two-door cabinet in my parents' bathroom. Midnight was shaking and I could see the whites of her eyes. Every once in a while she would move, then whimper, then scream. Then she was perfectly silent, like she was gone. It was so dark in there.

I didn't open the door to pet her. I don't remember if I spoke through the wooden slats to try to soothe her. I just know that she died. Her back was broken. I don't know if she died in the closet or if she was euthanized at the hospital, but I do remember seeing my father's face filled with tears. I'd never seen him cry. My parents told us that the doctor thought that Midnight had slipped a disc while hiding under the bed. A metal slat on the bed frame had probably pushed into her back, dislodged a disc, and broken her spine.

I decided that fear had killed her. If you run and hide, you die. Her death triggered something dark in me. Because all I wanted to do, just about every day, was run and hide.

Sunset

April 18, 1996

My mom pulled into the garage with one swooping motion, all of it so familiar, as if the movement of our car back into its spot was encoded in my blood. I'd done it so many times, and so many times I'd felt something unnamable and complex—raging fear and love and sorrow all twirled into one black knot in my belly.

She killed the engine, pulled the keys from the ignition and rounded the front of the car before I could even blink. She said something as she entered the house, cheerful words I couldn't discern as I pushed open the passenger door and rested my feet on the oil-stained garage floor. I was struck frozen by the sound of the screen door slapping shut. It was a noise that brought back three words: *Everyone hates you.* I heard this like an angry, menacing, shouting crowd. I wondered if I was losing my mind, actually hearing voices now. There was the smell of gasoline and fresh-cut grass. My bedroom was next to the garage and I could see the flowered wallpaper from my spot in the passenger seat. I did not want to go back into that room. I paused, my hands clammy in my lap, as the seared-in memory of my brother knocking down my bedroom door played behind my eyes.

My mom asked, "You coming in?" She passed quickly, opening the back hatch of the car, then limping my sloppily packed suitcase into the house. Our cocker spaniel, Cinder, now thirteen, snuck out of the busted hole in the screen door and ran to me. She was sweet and small, but she left anxiety urine in secret corners. Her stumpy tail wagged into a blur and I came back to the moment, took a few small shuffling steps, and bent down to touch her. She whimpered, kissed my ear, sending a chill down my spine, a desperately needed hit of adrenaline.

My dad was still at work. Surely he'd heard that his only daughter was coming home, that she'd (thank god) left that awful, dirty, too-crowded city. My father, a lover of Midwestern expansiveness, was proud to call New York City "the smallest city he'd ever been to," because when he visited, his hotel rooms were consistently minuscule.

I followed Cinder into the house and straight into my room, to my pink and green floral wallpaper, white wicker furniture, bookshelves filled with track trophies and stuffed animals. I had spent so many nights in this room dreading the next day. It was in this room that I'd sought refuge. It was in that closet that, as a teenager, I'd flown into an uncontrollable rage and broken everything in sight, pulling the rod and shelves out of the wall, my mom too scared to enter the room until the noise stopped. It was in that bed that I stayed awake at night wondering why I felt so much when everyone around me seemed to feel so little. And here I was again, back to this spot where the dark energy seemed inherent. I was back to the falling-in feeling, back to trying like hell to make it through the next hour. I was back to this one question: *What is wrong with me?*

I sat down on the edge of my bed like I'd broken several bones. Cinder jumped up next to me, sat down, and pressed her side into mine. I put my arm around her and held her chest with my palm, and the beating of her heart took me one shade out of the darkness. I held on to her as long as she would allow before my mom called, "Cinder, outside!" The backyard's screened-in porch door slammed. Cinder wiggled out of my grasp and trotted out of my room, her stubby tail twirling, her toenails clicking down the tile hallway.

I watched from my bedroom as my mom walked out to the patio outside my window, her black cardigan sweater pulled tight across her chest, her arms folded. She was taking a deep breath, searching the sky. It seemed she was whispering a prayer.

She came back inside, walked to the threshold of my bedroom, and suggested I rest while she made dinner. I opened my bedroom window and inhaled, noting the familiar scent of our forest, green and thick with its spring bounty. But I felt as if I were buzzing, like every fiber in my body was still surging with feedback from Manhattan. My ears rang. My head felt so full that I imagined it could've been riddled with tumors. I sat staring out the window and watched the sun disappear. The moon was full, as full as I'd ever seen it, like it was a balloon about to explode. I watched it rise through the trees in our backyard, inching ever so slowly to the tips of their branches like fingertips holding up the white ball. I sat there thinking that maybe this was all hormonal. Maybe I was just too connected to the moon. Maybe I'd spend my life going crazy every full moon, losing my mind until the new moon came and let me be.

Soon my mom called, "Dinner!" in the voice I'd heard each night around seven o'clock for eighteen years. My hands shook slightly at the dinner table. We ate without talking, then cleared the plates. I found myself mirroring my mother's chipper attitude as I loaded the dishes she'd rinsed. For this moment, I felt content returning home to the familiar, well-lit kitchen with the clean floor, the double oven, the welcoming tan and brown tiles. The house smelled of spaghetti with meat sauce and melted butter on baked potatoes. Cornhusks sat limp next to the stove; small bright-yellow dots of corn pollen marked the countertop.

My mom started the dishwasher, then sighed deeply, wiped her hands, turned off the lights in the kitchen, walked to the couch, and turned on the television. I dried my hands on the old baby-blue dishrag we'd had for decades and watched her from the darkened kitchen. She curled up on the couch and pulled a blanket over her lap as my thoughts pinged about. I had envisioned her wanting to talk, because she knew I wanted to talk. I wanted her to know what had gone so terribly wrong that I fell apart in Manhattan. I wanted a heart-to-heart. Her silence left me confused. Did she know something I didn't? Was my fallout in that apartment nothing to worry about? Again I tried to remember if I'd actually said the word *breakdown*. Yes, I had. Had I? Maybe I was wrong. Maybe it wasn't a breakdown but just a really bad day. Why weren't we talking about it?

She got up during a commercial break, went to her bedroom, and came back in her pajamas and robe, grinning but not making eye contact. She tied her robe's belt around her waist before sitting down with her feet folded underneath her. The way she didn't look at me told me that there would be no conversation.

At about ten o'clock, as I drifted in and out of sleep on the couch, my dad came home from work. I heard the swish of the door to the garage opening, his dress shoes clicking down the hall-way, his briefcase hitting the floor, his walk to the coat closet. Every single night, before doing anything, he hung up his coat. I heard the hush of fabric, the clank of the metal hanger on the rod, and then the closet door swinging shut. This night, after the routine was over, I imagined he would go into the kitchen and grab his already-plated cold dinner and start eating, or maybe go change out of his suit and tie into his casual after-work clothes.

He did neither of those rituals. Instead, he walked over to me, sat down practically on top of me, hugged me tight, held both my hands, and said in a gentle voice, "How ya doin'?" A wave of his cologne hit me and the contrast of my mom's avoidance versus my dad nearly enveloping me was disorienting. Initially, I felt smoth-ered, uncomfortable. Then, when I took my eyes away from the floor and looked into his, tears came. The emotion gathered in my throat and began to block my wind. He shook his head and pulled me in for a long, tight hug. I cried audibly, then hysterically, and he held on to me.

His attention helped me let go a little. I knew nothing except that I needed to let go. I had to stop fighting this darkness. As I hugged my dad, I took my hand away from my eyes and saw my mom, who had turned off the television and was crying too.

It was then that I understood. She was shedding the tears of a mother who was terrified, with no idea what to do or say. She wasn't turning on the television out of carelessness or anger. Rather, she didn't understand what had left me lying deadened on my apartment floor in New York City. She was scared that if she said the wrong thing, or probed too deeply, I would shut down forever. My dad's arrival, his ability to risk reaching out to me, to help me feel something, brought tears of relief to her.

This was our pattern. My father could look into my eyes and see that something troubled me. When he was home, his radar for my emotional well-being was spot on. He saved me so many times as a child, pulling me aside and saying, "You okay?" as soon as he saw the shadows cross my eyes. The problem was that he was at work most of my waking hours. It was as if I had a lifeline that was there, but out of reach. Always so busy.

My dad held on to me as I wept, but my arms went limp and my face numb. My mom cradled one of my hands in both of hers and nodded as my dad repeated, quietly, over and over: "It's going to be okay, Julie. It's going to be okay."

"What happened?" my dad said. In his words, I heard: *Who did this to you? What is broken and how can I fix it?*

"Nothing happened," I said. I didn't say that for weeks I'd imagined jumping in front of oncoming traffic or stepping onto the third rail. I couldn't say that at that moment I fantasized about swallowing every pill in the house. "I can't think. I hate being... I just hate being. I could just sleep until I die. I just can't do this."

"Do what, honey?" my Mom asked gently.

"Be," I said.

It is hard to be a puppy. Your siblings are just as hungry as you, just as uncoordinated, also deaf and blind. You're not really a dog yet—you're just longing. You're just hunger. If you can manage to find your way to a teat, you'll most likely get pushed over by the bigger, hungrier sibling who, just like you, is simply trying to survive.

Sometimes puppies wander off, wobble away from their mother, off the whelping blanket and onto the cold, hard ground. That's when the mama dog gets up, walks over, gently picks up her wayward child, and brings him back to his family. Back to their nest on the blanket, where warmth and nourishment can be found.

The Wrong Dog, New York City

Early Spring 1996

In the midst of the heartbreak with Will, before I collapsed on the floor, I decided to get a dog. If Will wouldn't love me, I reasoned, a dog might. Our building allowed dogs and the landlord seemed unfazed by the question. Leah had reluctantly agreed that if the dog was my responsibility, we could get one. We'd already gotten a small gray rabbit—but she bit and didn't have a single readable emotion. I bought a leash for her and took her out to East 82nd Street. She froze in fear and then crapped on the sidewalk.

Leah was away for the weekend when I walked up to the animal shelter on Second Avenue, praying I'd find comfort in a dog the way I had as a child. I opened the door to the shelter and introduced myself to the woman at the counter, expressing my interest in adopting a dog. She was Latina with beautiful skin and a kind smile. She handed me a form to fill out, and we chatted politely as I wrote down my address, place of employment, and living situation. "I've always had a dog." I said. " Always. It just feels so strange not having one right now."

She nodded deeply. "I know!" she said. "Walking into a house where there's no little wagging tail to greet you just feels plain wrong. I have three." I nodded and laughed, tears brimming. The last thing I wanted was to cry here, now, so I pretended to sneeze and closed my eyes, then wiped them with a tissue.

I handed her the form and she looked it over. "Great," she said, scanning the information. "You work full time?" She looked concerned.

"Well, I work from home a day or two a week." Total lie. "I'm a writer so I work out of my apartment a lot." Another total lie.

She smiled at me. "Jealous!" she said, laughing. "Geez, lucky you. Do you have any other pets currently?"

"No," I said, shaking my head, completely, honestly forgetting about the rabbit.

"Well, looks great. Come on back. Let's look at some of these dogs." She asked what size dog I wanted and I indicated that I usually liked bigger dogs. "With your handling experience, we could probably match you with one of our big guys. Oh! I know! I have the perfect big girl for you." I stood blissed out by her confidence in me and shoved my hands in my pockets in an attempt to not appear weirdly enthusiastic.

She sent me to the space where they introduce dogs to potential owners. The room was all concrete, the floor painted purple, the walls a vivid orange. A heavyset trainer with short hair and royal-blue clogs entered and introduced herself as Rita. She told me a bit about a dog they thought might be good for me. "She's a total goofy love," she said. "She's not at all aggressive, has some basic obedience training, and just needs a bit more time and a good home." I sat there thinking, *She just needs a good home. She just needs love. I can give her love.*

My front-desk friend opened the door and in came an enormous gray dog that looked to be part mastiff, part bulldog. I felt no immediate connection but was so happy when the dog came to sniff me, her tail twirling. I cooed, smiled, laughed, and let her lick my cheek before saying I'd take her. I quickly signed the papers, coughed up a hundred bucks and was soon walking down Second Avenue behind my new ninety-five-pound dog.

At my apartment door, I struggled with the lock as the dog yanked on the leash. I pulled her into the entryway, already worried that this was a mistake. It felt like I was walking a pony into my 750-square-foot apartment. When the door to the place swung open, the leash went taut as the dog lunged straight at the rabbit's cage. She started barking madly, drooling, clawing the hardwood floor. I dragged the dog downstairs to the bedroom and tried to calm her. She continued to lunge for the stairs but eventually became interested in the scents on the pile of dirty clothes on my bedroom floor. She walked to my bed and jumped up, her dirty paws leaving dusty prints on my pillowcases.

"Shhhh," I said. "Shhhhh, it's okay." She looked at me, not with anxiety or fear, but with blankness. It seemed as if she'd gone into a shallow, shifty-eyed, fearful state. After all, I'd taken her into my nearly windowless bedroom and wouldn't let her leave. Who knew what she'd been through prior to meeting me? I turned on some quiet music, trying to get her to calm down and forget about the bunny she knew was just one floor above. I lay down and invited her to come onto the bed with me. She frantically sniffed everything, as if searching for more traces of edible animals.

"Come here, girl," I said, in my sweetest voice. "Come on the bed. Hop up." I patted the sheets and she obliged. I told her to sit, to lie down, and she half did. Rigid, she lay on the bed with me for about four seconds, and in those few heartbreaking beats, I realized that what I wanted, more than this dog, more than anything, was the weight of someone next to me in my bed. I wanted to be held. I wanted Will.

She never lay down. Instead she popped up and darted toward the door again, barking. I knew I'd made a terrible mistake. I couldn't keep this dog. I imagined that the whole world hated me for what I'd just done. I put the dog's leash back on, opened the door, and tried to keep my balance as she clawed her way toward the rabbit's cage, her hackles up, her lips flapping and spewing drool. "No!" I yelled, pulling with all my might. "Jesus Christ." I dragged her out of the apartment and back up Second Avenue.

The shelter was preparing to close when I opened the door and walked back in with the dog. My front-desk confidante looked at me, surprised. "Forget something?" she asked.

I couldn't look at her. "I can't keep her. I'm so sorry." The dog was panting, her bloodshot eyes darting around the lobby.

My front-desk friend looked at me like I'd just sprouted a second head. "What? Why not?"

"I forgot about my roommate's rabbit," I said, another complete lie. "He practically ate it in one bite."

"The dog is a *she*," she said, snatching the leash from me.

"I'm sorry," I said. "I'm so sorry."

She sighed. "Let me call Rita to take her back to her cage. Now I've got to process your refund." She looked at her watch.

"I don't want a refund," I said, still not making eye contact. "Just keep it. I'm so sorry." I ran out the door, back down Second Avenue, distraught. I shuddered at the thought of what I'd just done, tried to force an enormous, terrified, overly stimulated animal to lie down in bed with me. I panicked, thinking that perhaps living in the city this past year, I'd lost my connection to animals and the natural world. If that happened, nothing could help me. No animal, no person, nothing. The sadness swallowed me as I walked back into my apartment and went to bed alone. I lay there promising myself that I would never, ever tell a soul what I'd just done.

The sorrow on that lonely walk back to my apartment was like the strike of lightning that cracked the dam. I didn't know this then, but depression can be like a slow leak. Once the dam's hit, water starts to seep through and as the days and weeks go by, the crack grows bigger.

I tried to search for the moon when I lived in Manhattan as a way to orient myself, to stem the tide of sorrow. But I could rarely find it. Sometimes I would see a sliver of a crescent through the crack of two buildings. I couldn't yet admit that I missed the wide-open spaces of Ohio, that I longed for a quiet night interrupted only by cricket song. In New York, I was mostly inside, underground even. Soon, I forgot to look up at all. And no matter how much you try, when the rising water starts to seep under your door, you can't keep pretending that your world is not flooding.

SINKING

APRIL 19, 1996

The first morning back in Ohio, I woke at 11 a.m., once again disoriented from a deadened sleep. I had slept for twelve hours, but felt like I'd merely blinked. I couldn't fathom ever getting out of bed.

At 11:30, I still lay in bed not moving. I had no idea what to do. Every move I made felt off, wrong, awkward, strange. I had felt some version of this malaise my whole life, but now it had officially taken over. I craved stillness, silence, and darkness. I spent much of that first morning in Ohio with a pillow over my face. I could not bear that I had failed in New York and returned to my childhood home.

Eventually I heard the gentle click of my mom opening my bedroom door. She tiptoed in with toast and juice, placing them quietly on my bedside table. I craved solitude and wanted her to leave. Instead she sat down on the edge of my bed and put her hand on my hip. The touch made me flinch.

"Honey?" she said.

"What," I mumbled. She pulled the pillow up a bit. I fought the urge to bat away her hand.

"I'm going out to lunch with Lynn Sears. I've had it planned for a while and I just can't cancel. Will you be okay?"

"Yes," I said, both annoyed and grateful that she was leaving. I wondered if she was imagining me tossing a hair dryer in the bathtub. "I'll be fine."

"So," she paused, as if what she was going to say next needed careful phrasing. "So ... what are you going to do today?"

In hindsight, I can see that she was doing all she could to be kind to me. A simple check-in. Just making conversation. But I picked up the pillow and threw it at her. She blocked it with her arm, but the corner of it smacked her cheek. I sneered and said, "Mom, just fucking go." She stood up, turned, and walked away.

I rolled over, shaking. This was our pattern. She showed up, and I punished her. She tried tenderness, but her well-intentioned attempts misfired. She had the distinct dishonor of perpetually saying the exact wrong thing, no matter the words, and suffering the wrath of my pain and anger.

As was her custom, she left silently, carefully. I heard her car pulling away followed by the thud of the garage door closing. Her departure brought a swirl of guilt, relief, and despair, enough emotion to lull me back into a deep, black sleep. What relief sleep had become. As I drifted down I wished with clear, longing intention to sleep for an eternity.

If fate works the way I think it does, I am pretty sure that at this point, my puppy was sleeping a lot too. His mama was licking his ears clean, her warm, dry tongue a lucky blanket. He could only suckle and sleep. It's not easy, the hard work of being a newborn puppy. He got stepped on, squished, beaten to the last available teat. He needed his mother desperately, and she was exhausted. He was blind and hungry, aided only by his nose toward the scent of sustenance. He could clumsily crawl, his eyes couldn't open, but he knew that if he stayed safe and warm with his family, if he slept as much as he needed to sleep, he would be okay.

I believe that when Bunker and I were both helpless against the challenges of life, when we both needed unconditional love or would die, our mothers showed up and did what mothers do. They do everything they can to save their children.

Blarney
1982

After Midnight died, my parents decided we should get a purebred puppy. We researched breeds and agreed that an Irish setter would be a good fit for our family. We brought Blarney home when I was about nine years old. She was a little nut-brown puppy, all legs and plate-wide feet, and she would curl up and sleep in the bend of my legs. In between random bursts of goofy puppy energy, she was quiet and timid, and I remember kissing her head, feeling the large bump on the crown of her skull as she looked at me as if I were an angel. I would brush her soft-as-down ears, the rusty orange fur turned rich maroon by her first birthday.

More than once, Clay noticed our connection, and in front of me, he would torment her—bump her, push her down so that her long, spindly legs splayed out in all four directions, her claws scratching the hardwood floor in resistance. But I also remember seeing him snuggle with her on the floor in front of the television when he thought I wasn't watching.

When we left the house, Blarney would sometimes try to escape and come with us. If successful, she would sprint to the end of our long driveway, then chase our car for a quarter-mile down the road while we yelled out the window, "No, Blarney! Go home!" She would lope through the grass, dodging mailboxes and trees, the whites of her eyes showing, her ears blown back, her body in a full sprint.

Once, when Blarney was two, my mom's station wagon pulled out of the garage, idled down the driveway, heading for the grocery store. I was standing in the kitchen making a snack when I noticed the red blur of Blarney's body galloping past the kitchen window.

I raced to the front door. "Blarney!" I yelled. My mom turned out of the driveway and Blarney ran, full speed, toward the road. I marveled at her power, at the capacity of her lungs to gather enough oxygen to supply her pumping blood. It was a beautiful sight, an Irish setter at full speed, ears back, tongue relaxed and out. She should've been in a sunny, open field with wildflowers and scurrying mice. Instead she was chasing my mom's station wagon, hoping to never be left behind, exactly as a school bus barreled past our driveway the moment she so gracefully, quickly, tried to cross.

I stopped halfway down the driveway and watched the bus crash into her body. Her head thwacked against the bus's grill, her sweet soft ears flailing wildly. Her body fell to the road and the bus drove over her before slowing to a stop.

I held my hands to my mouth to feel if the screaming I heard was actually coming from my body. I began to run, full speed to the end of my driveway. The kids on the bus were clambering to the back window to gawk at my beloved dog. The driver stood up, opened the door, and walked down two of the stairs, but didn't step onto the road. I paused at the end of my driveway, twenty feet from where Blarney's body lay, and didn't realize my mom had stopped her car until she came up to me and grabbed my wrists. She yelled at me to stop screaming.

"Breathe, Julie," she yelled. "Breathe!" All I could do was scream. I wanted to go to Blarney, but my mom held me back. She motioned to the bus driver to move on. When the bus pulled away, I screamed, "The bus is *leaving*! They ran over Blarney and they're leaving! Mom! Call the police! They can't just *leave!*"

Mrs. Rankins, the elderly widow who lived alone across the road from us, had come outside. She never liked Blarney, would shoo her out of her yard with a broom. She stood at the end of her driveway, arms tightly crossed. She was small with cropped black hair, always looking out her window with a disapproving grimace.

"Mrs. Rankins," my mom said, calling over to her. "Can you please take Julie while I rush Blarney to the vet?" I looked at my mom with shock.

"No, Mom! I want to go with you! I'll hold Blarney in the back seat. You drive." I wanted to be with Blarney if she were in pain or were to die. I needed to be with her, to comfort her. She was hurt; I was hurt. She was scared; I was scared. She could not die without my telling her that the world was good, that she'd done good, that I loved her. I could not fathom being absent from her traumatic injury or death.

"Julie," my Mom said. "Go." She pointed to Mrs. Rankins' house.

"But, I can't not be there!" I screamed. My mother wanted to protect me; she didn't understand that I felt that Blarney was *mine*. She was my love, my solace in this family I didn't understand. I couldn't let her die without me.

I wasn't given a choice. Mrs. Rankins held my forearm and led me up her driveway. "You can't see that, dear," she said. I barely knew Mrs. Rankins. The image of Blarney's body hitting the bus and falling to the road looped endlessly in my mind. I found myself silenced. The tears stopped abruptly. My lips tingled. I stole a glimpse of one of the neighbor boys putting Blarney's limp body into the back of my mom's station wagon. Blarney's head dangled, inert, lifeless.

After my mom drove away, Mrs. Rankins took me inside her house that smelled like mothballs and disinfectant. Everything was dark brown: the carpet, the walls, the rug, the stove, the refrigerator. She offered me graham crackers and milk, and I took them without words and waited for my mom to return.

When the doorbell finally rang, I went to the door behind Mrs. Rankins and knew immediately when the door revealed a sliver of my mom's face that Blarney was gone. She had died; I had missed it.

I remember watching my father cry that night as he played piano. Our whole family separated during the mourning. We ate alone, we wept alone, and we went to bed early. Later that night, I lay in bed reeling. Through the wall, I heard Clay crying. I held up my knuckle, thinking about knocking, if only to indicate to him that I felt sad too. Chances were he'd shout an obscenity through the drywall, but I took that risk and pulled my fingers down, then rapped them gently, three times. Silence. No longer the sound of our big, beautiful dog bounding down the hall. Then, when I thought it was past all hope, three knocks back.

LAKE BEAUCHÊNE, QUÉBEC
MAY 1996

A few hours after I threw the pillow at my mom, she returned from her lunch and found me still in bed. She walked into my room, opened the windows, and left without saying a word. I appreciated her silence and the fresh air, the sound of the wind in the trees, the birds singing. Nature thrived in the forest outside my bedroom window, and life could go on while I slumbered. It really didn't matter if I was there or not. The earth would turn, the sun would rise, the moon would wax and wane. I found the continuity consoling and further proof that I need not be alive.

Hunger eventually pulled me out of bed and I went to the kitchen to pour a bowl of cereal. I ate sleepily at the kitchen table, and my mom sat across from me. The clock read 1:30 p.m. She had a cup of coffee and the newspaper. I didn't know what day it was, whether my mom had called in sick or it was a weekend.

"Lynn says hi," she said, before taking a long sip of her black coffee. "She's glad you're home. She lived in New York for a few years and said she couldn't leave soon enough." I stared blankly at the wall, swallowing a pang of defensiveness for Manhattan. Part of me loved New York—the energy, the potential, the noise. "Oh, and Dad called," she said, holding the newspaper in front of her face. "He's looking into taking you up to Lake Beauchêne in a few weeks."

Lake Beauchêne was a remote fishing preserve in Québec that my dad loved. He had taken Clay there every summer for the past few years. Sometimes my parents went with friends. I'd never been. The last time my dad and brother went to the lakes, they took my brother's friend and his terminally ill father. This man, who had only a few weeks to live, wanted to spend some of his final days on these sacred waters in a boat with his son, to say words only the two of them and the loons would ever hear. I thought this was so beautiful and tragic, and I understood Lake Beauchêne to be the kind of place for special conversations.

I also knew that this would be my dad's attempt at an *I'll Save Julie* trip, but I didn't care. I was up for being saved. It was a thirteen-hour drive, and I wanted thirteen hours alone with my dad. I needed some time with him on a boat. I needed to be in a remote place with no interruptions, no work, just trees, birds, fishing gear, and my father's ear. I longed to hear the loons calling through the morning fog.

"Do you think fishing might be something you'd want to do?" my mom asked. I noted her overly careful wording.

"Sure, whatever," I said. She pulled the newspaper down, squinted at me over her reading glasses, smiled slightly, and offered to take my empty cereal bowl. "Thanks," I said, as I heaved myself up out of the chair and to the couch, where I disappeared into the television. I spent some time with MTV, then looked for a cheesy movie to watch. I stumbled upon *Some Kind of Wonderful* and curled into the couch, blissful at the escape.

The next several days resembled this one. I slept past noon and my mom tiptoed around me offering food and silence as I lay on the couch, watched television, and slept. I was grateful for her patience and quiet with me. She was the one who rescued me from my urban demise, and the next day I threw a pillow at her. She had every right to be angry with me, but she wasn't.

Dad booked our fishing trip for the next week. For at least a few days I could escape my suffocating bedroom. Early the following Saturday morning, Dad and I packed the car while Mom fussed over the cooler and its peanut butter and jelly sandwiches, chips, apples, chocolate chip cookies, and soda. I was having another tough day, my thoughts running dark, but I managed to put enough underwear in a bag and get into the passenger seat of the car.

After pulling onto the freeway, my dad and I started talking. Since my returning home, aside from the night he held me as I cried, we hadn't spoken much. He was mostly working; I was mostly sleeping.

So in his car, on Route 71 North, he asked what happened with Will. I told him that I'd fallen deeply in love but that Will was fighting some demons. I told my dad that I would always love Will and that he was a good man. My dad told me he thought the guy was too negative and that I was better off. I smiled and watched the road.

The truth was, Will had started calling around the second week I was home. "I miss you," he'd say. "More than I thought I would. I miss your skin. No one has skin like yours. So soft. No one else kisses me the way you do." Of course I knew that he'd been with other women both while I was in New York and since I'd left, and I was aware enough to recognize that he loved me partially because I'd made myself unattainable. But I desperately needed to be wanted. I needed to feel adored and part of me still loved him, so I answered his calls late at night in my bedroom. I told him that I missed him and didn't understand why things hadn't worked out between us. He hinted that maybe some day they still could, but I couldn't ever imagine that.

Each mile out of Ohio peeled off another layer of the malaise. It felt like leaving New York: leaving trouble behind. I made a mental note that I needed to be careful, because I could get used to running away. Somewhere past the Canadian border, as we skirted around the lip of Lake Ontario, our tank nearing empty, we stopped at a gas station, and I started driving. As I pulled onto the freeway, my dad said, "Can I tell you about my parents' deaths?" The question startled me. I glanced at him and nodded.

My father was with both his parents when they died. His mother died when he was only twenty-four, before Clay or I was even born. She had rheumatic heart disease—a result of her childhood rheumatic fever. Her heart was literally too big for her chest. She died in the hospital with my father watching, scared. My grandfather and father loved her so dearly for her unfailing grace, her lilting smile, her gentle demeanor in the face of the harshness of a Depression-era life. My dad was in law school when she died, and he struggled to focus. He and my mom had been married for only two years and they lived in a small rental house in Ithaca, New York. My dad mourned his mom's passing between the pages of law books, trying to wrap his mind around two difficult styles of cognition: the law and how to live without his mother.

After my grandmother died, every now and then, without warning, my grandfather would show up on my parents' doorstep. My dad would open the door expecting a classmate but instead he'd find his father, skin ashen, spirit weakened. He had driven straight from Illinois to New York just to see his son. My dad would motion for his father to enter, and inside, they'd shake hands firmly, then hug for a long while. My mom would whip up a quick dinner and they'd sit down together, around a table, talking. My grandfather would smile at the life his son was building, scratch their beagle behind the ears, and pat his lap so the dog would join him.

My father and his father would sit on the couch and talk. For hours. Grandpa would reminisce about life, about Grandma, about having to put down Marty, his overweight and elderly beagle, soon after his wife died. My father says that these were some of the most loving and poignant times he'd ever had with his father. Grandpa talked, Dad listened, and they cried together. Quietly in one of those conversations, Grandpa said, "You know what I am doing, don't you, son?" My dad listened intently to his father's soft words. "I am grieving. And I know this will pass, because time heals all things."

I understood, as I drove, that my father was telling me this story so that I might know that he and my ancestors had suffered too, and we all deal with emotional pain in our own ways. The solidarity I felt with my father's and grandfather's pain was more consolation than anything I'd felt for years, but still—the nagging fact remained. They were sad from death; I was sad from life.

My grandfather had endured unimaginable hardship. His mother told him he was unwanted and kicked him out at age nine. He lived on the streets, worked odd jobs for food, just trying to survive. He fist-fought other homeless boys. A lot. He delivered newspapers in the dead of an Illinois winter with shoes that had holes in them. A woman inside one of the fancier houses on his paper route gave him her daughter's old heeled lace-up shoes. He accepted them with gratitude, not caring that he was a young boy wearing girls' shoes. He was just glad his feet were covered. He never forgot that thoughtful woman.

Despite everything, somehow my grandfather began to learn how to navigate difficult times with love. He understood that focusing on all that was kind and gentle, empathic and wise, would give him strength. His strength turned out to be a gift that would last our family for generations. But I feared it had skipped me.

As we drove through the forested plains of southern Québec, my father tolerated my playing endless amounts of Ani DiFranco. We were in the middle of nowhere, the only car for miles, when he asked, "Can I tell you the story of when my father died now?" I squeezed the steering wheel and nodded.

My grandfather was stricken with lung cancer around 1978. My dad was thirty-three; I was five and my brother eight. My father was already immersed in his legal work, and I wonder now if focusing on work helped him not miss his mother so much. Perhaps his job was a perfect diversion from his loss.

In August 1978, as my grandfather's cancer progressed, it became clear that he had only a matter of days left. So my father left his office and drove alone to the hospital in Canton, Illinois, to sit next to my grandfather's bed. After only a few days, it was clear the end was near. As my grandfather struggled to talk, the nurses warned that he might not make it through the night. Grandpa was having great difficulty breathing; his skin was damp and gray. All night, my father sat next to his hero, the man who always told him how loved he was, how talented he was, how he could do anything if he worked hard enough. "One more breath, Dad. One more breath," my father begged. It became a plea. "Please, Dad. One more breath. Please." My grandfather was laboring terribly, and my father held his hands, clutched them with fervor, the last remnant of his immediate family quickly slipping away. As dawn approached and the top of the sun touched the horizon, my father started reciting the 23rd Psalm. "The Lord is my Shepherd; I shall not want..." He recited the final stanza, his throat constricted with emotion. "Surely goodness and mercy shall follow me all the days of my life, And I will dwell in the House of the Lord forever."

After my father spoke these final words, my grandfather passed. This last breath brought blood, lots of blood, out of his mouth, and my traumatized father walked right out of the hospital room. He told me about how he walked outside just after sunrise, like he didn't know how to go on. But then he remembered his father's drives to Ithaca, and he continued walking. He walked the entire length and breadth of Canton, Illinois, devastated. The sun reached the top of the sky at noon, and he was still walking, unsure how to continue with this day and all the days that would follow. I wonder now if he decided during that walk that work would be his consolation. Work was constant. It would not die. It would not ever go away. It would sustain him, and even provide for his wife and children.

Our car sped along the two-lane Canadian road, and my father cried. His chest heaved with sobs. I struggled to focus on the road, considered pulling over, but could tell that he didn't want me to stop. He wanted me to keep driving, to keep moving, to keep listening. He wanted me to know that I wasn't the only one who had felt devastating pain.

He told me that his father taught him about kindness, unconditional love, family, and persistence. He'd given him the gifts of music and nature and sports. He'd taught him how to express himself wholly and completely, and the morning his father died, my dad walked along the weedy sidewalks, patchwork fields of soybean and corn in the distance, with a hollow in his chest that he hoped would be filled some day by the love of his new family and cherished memories of his mother and father.

I cried too as I drove, blinking to maintain visibility. The thought of losing one parent when I was twenty-four and the other at thirty-three terrified me. How did my father survive this? I began to understand more deeply his love for my mother, for her steady nature, her ability to wake up each morning with a smile.

We shared a silent few miles, my hand in his. I loved so very much that I had a man in my life who was not afraid to cry. My dad embraced emotion. He felt it deeply. Up surged a pang of regret that when I was a young child, feeling so much, he wasn't home to tell me that my sadness wasn't a sign of weakness. I felt this discomfort, then shut it down. He was trying so hard to help, and there was no way I could tell him now how much his absences had affected me.

Our first morning at the lakes, we rose early in our little brown cabin at the water's edge. As I'd hoped, the loons were calling. It was hard to see them, but their mournful cries resonated deeply. It was as if they were saying, "Come. Come onto our sacred waters. Bring your sadness. We will take it from you." My dad prepared the rods and lures, grabbed the map, and held my hand as I stepped into the boat. We were pulling away from the dock as the sun poked the edge of the horizon. He steered the boat out to the narrows between Beauchêne and Little Beauchêne, the two main lakes. The water shone like glass below us, teeming with fish we couldn't see.

We fished without much success, but we didn't care. Our rods resting on the boat's edge, I told him about Brian, my first college boyfriend, and many of the feelings that still swirled around in me about that first love. I told him about Will and about how our relationship had seemed so hopeful before it fell apart. Eventually, I told him about the miserable way I had lost my virginity at age seventeen. I saw sorrow in my father's eyes, and I felt him struggling to understand.

After we ate lunch from the cooler, the warm sun sparkled on the water, and we were lulled into a peaceful slumber in the palm of the lake. We woke up when the boat drifted into a large fallen tree limb. The hull bumped hard against the branch and we were both so startled and confused by the echoing sound that we shot upright. His hair was sticking straight up, his sunglasses crooked on the end of his nose. Who knows how odd I looked; I hadn't showered since Ohio. We found the sight of each other hysterically funny and laughed until our sides ached. Later, after more fishing, we sped back to the dock, hungry for dinner in the main cabin. In the rush of wind and oxygen, I remembered for a quick moment what happy felt like.

Based on a wisp of a story that the breeder told us, we can piece together that right about the time I was docking that boat, Bunker was experiencing his own rush of wind, water, and oxygen. All of the puppies, now about six weeks old, had escaped out the unlocked laundry-room door. They'd taken off through the woods beyond the farmhouse, down to the river. The nice lady didn't notice until dusk, when she came home from the grocery store, noticed the quiet, and opened the door to discover an empty whelping room. Not one dog to be found.

The breeder told us that all the dogs had followed Bunker's father, like he was the damned pied piper, down to Raccoon Creek, across the road, and down the steep hill to the spot where the older dogs sometimes romped while the nice people in the house took a swim. This was an unauthorized trip, though, and soon the nice lady was stomping through the woods, her flashlight beaming a jump rope of light through the trees. "Hunter!" she yelled at the papa dog. "You get your butt up here!" Hunter raced toward her.

The puppies followed, most of them, and she clipped them all onto leashes. Two pups lagged behind. She had to wade ankle-deep into the muddy water to gather Bunker and his bigger brother. Those two, she said, were too busy to obey her commands, romping in the gloaming, covered in mud and giddy with discovery.

Rhythm Is Gonna Get You

Fall 1988

Clay attended the all-boys high school in Columbus. It was the school with which my all-girls school had dances, proms, parties, and football games. Clay was popular; I was not. The popular girls at my school always found it strange that my brother and I were related. That is, until our first high school party. Another brother-sister pair with the same senior-freshman split was hosting and invited us both. Lots of the popular girls from my class would be there—and I desperately wanted to be part of that crowd.

My parents forced Clay to let me come with him so I teased my permed hair to unadvisable heights, carefully lined my lips with red liner before adding shimmery light-pink gloss, then donned my acid-washed skinny jeans with the exposed buttons and my red, blue, and yellow chunky striped sweater. I slid on some penny loafers (with shiny pennies inserted) and was ready. Clay was waiting for me in the car, honking at me as I rushed to jump into the passenger seat. Dad let us take his awesome sports car, the maroon Mazda RX-7.

My stomach twirled as we pulled up to the party. Clay walked into the house ahead of me, heading to the kitchen and high-fiving his buddies. I stood in the entryway, shifting my weight from one foot to the other, not sure where to go.

A bass beat emanated from downstairs. Down the half-dozen steps was a sunken living room with a couch and chair facing the television and stereo. The far wall of the living room had sliding glass doors that led out to a patio. There sat a hot tub, the hot water twirling steam into the cool night.

The popular girls from my school stood in the corner, huddled like hair-sprayed football players. They turned to me, and said, "Oh, hi!" They gave my outfit the once-over and I did a half wave with my elbow pinned to my body. I approached, which could've gone terribly wrong, but they pulled out of their huddle and gave me half-body hugs. Kathy, our school's richest and most popular girl, asked if I was excited about coming to the party, like I was a five-year-old. I smiled and nodded, like a five-year-old.

The stereo was blasting 97.9, WNCI. That was my station. I knew just about every song they played. I had danced alone in my room for hours to their music, went jogging with my Walkman tuned to only that frequency. Once, I even called in and was the 97th caller, and won tickets to a Prince concert, the Lovesexy tour. As the girls chatted, I smiled and tapped my toe to "Nothing's Gonna Stop Us Now" by Starship.

Two of the senior boys came down the stairs and walked outside, then stripped down to their boxers and stepped into the hot tub. Kathy walked to the sliding glass doors and yelled out to them, "You *guys!* We're not supposed to get into the hot tub until we're smashed! You can't already be drunk, can you?" She laughed as they lowered themselves into the steaming water, nodding and smiling.

"Oh, my god," she said, grabbing my forearm. "Those guys are hammered and it's not even nine o'clock!" I couldn't believe that the popular girl was touching me, laughing with me at a party.

"They could drown!" I said, and she looked at me, her eyes wide, laughing. I smiled like I'd meant to make a joke. The radio was blasting a commercial, then the DJ said something unintelligible before we heard the unmistakable cowbell-synthesizer beat that begins George Michael's "I Want Your Sex." The girls started screaming and jumping up and down and Maddie grabbed my hand and we moved out to the open space in the living room and started dancing.

I barely danced, afraid the boys were watching us. Clay was still upstairs with his friends, and the boys in the hot tub weren't paying attention. So I laughed and smiled as the girls hopped up and down with their eyes closed. Maddie and Kathy were good dancers, but Diane and Renee looked ridiculous. I was astounded, both by their lack of rhythm and by their apparent lack of self-consciousness.

"C-C-C-C-C-C'mon!" We all sang together. I felt my body loosening up. Someone turned off the lights and all the girls screamed. I relaxed a little and did a few of the moves that I'd practiced in my room—some serious hip shaking followed by a tip of the toes twirl. When I finished, all the girls yelled, "Go, Julie! Woohoo!" I laughed, feeling half embarrassed, half thrilled. I kept going and soon it was like I was alone in my room, dancing with the lights low and the music blaring. Except I was with friends, actual friends, who loved to dance just like me.

Thirty minutes into the dancing, I was thinking that if this was what high school parties were like, I was in. I knew all of the words to these songs, and the other girls watched me lip sync, watched my moves, and tried to imitate them, and it was as if I could feel my social status rising with each shake of my hips.

When the station played Belinda Carlisle's "Heaven Is a Place on Earth," we all sang the first few lines as loud as we could. "*Ooh baby, do you know what that's worth? Ooh, heaven is a place on earth. They say in heaven, love comes first. We'll make heaven a place on earth!*" I was breathless with laughter, dancing with abandon. I couldn't remember having this much fun. Ever. In my entire life.

Soon, the boys from the hot tub came in and started dancing with us, their boxers dripping. I thought that was great. I had no concept of sex yet. I had no idea that things on dance floors could lead to anything but the need for an ice cold lemonade and a snack. As far as I was concerned, everything was great. The whole world was an amazing, wonderful place because of this half-lit living room with the popular girls (and me!) dancing along to Belinda and George and Whitney. Soon the dance floor was the place to be, and I was dripping with sweat. We all were. I wanted to dance all night. This was so easy, so amazing. Sometimes a girlfriend and

I would hug and jump up and down, hold hands and try to do the same move. Sometimes a boy would put his body against my back and we'd sway together. I loved the way this felt. Something beautiful was awakening in me. I did my best Axl Rose interpretation (which was spot-on, by the way) and laughed so hard I nearly cried.

At one point, during Duran Duran's "Notorious," I noticed Clay standing across the room watching me. I waved at him and motioned for him to join us. He looked away, then turned his back toward me. Whatever. I didn't care. "No-No-Notorious!" We screamed. I felt beautiful. I felt like I belonged. I noticed some of the boys watching me dance, and for the first time in my young teenage life, I honestly thought I might be pretty.

I had to pee during Madonna's "Open Your Heart," so I trotted up the stairs to find the bathroom. Clay followed me and grabbed my wrist and said, "Let's go. We're leaving."

"Why?" I asked. I checked my watch. It was only 11:30. We'd been there for less than three hours. Our parents told us to leave at midnight. "We don't have to leave for another half-hour." I was out of breath, giddy from dancing, and eager to get back downstairs.

"Well, I'm going," he said. "And I'm your ride. So come on."

"Please?" I said. "Can we stay just a little bit longer? I love this song!"

"You are ridiculous. Godammit!" he yelled. "Come outside and get in the fucking car right now."

"But I have to pee," I said, ignoring his foul mood and pondering letting him leave without me.

"Hurry the fuck up, then," he said, holding the front door open.

"Okay! Okay!" I said, my hands up in surrender as I sidled into the powder room. I peed and sang, "*I'll hold the lock and you'll hold the key. Open your heart to me-e-e,*" then came out into the foyer and asked if I could go say good-bye to my new friends.

"No," he said. "We're leaving."

I heard George Michael's "Faith" coming on and said, "Oh, man. Please? One more song? Can we stay? Pleeease?"

"I'm leaving," he said, walking out the door. He slammed it hard. I didn't know how I'd get home without him, so I followed him outside and got in the car. I should've been mad, but I was still too happy from the great party, out of breath, damp with sweat.

We sat in the car for a while, and he didn't put the key into the ignition. He had his hands on the steering wheel, and he was looking down into his lap. I was about to ask him what he was doing when he began speaking through clenched teeth.

"You...looked...like a *fucking* hobag." Spit flew out of his mouth with those last two words. I had no idea what a hobag was. I wondered if he meant hobo.

"What?" I said.

"What the fuck do you think you were doing in there?" he said. I was scared now. He was a senior, had been going to these kinds of parties for at least four years, and he knew how to act. Clearly I'd done something uncool.

"I have no idea what you're talking about," I said, trying to sound strong.

"You are so full of shit. You do too."

"No. Honestly. I don't."

He paused, squeezed the steering wheel, and then said, "You looked like a big, huge whore. A slut. I am so fucking embarrassed right now. I can't fucking *believe* what you were doing in there. You should be glad I got you out of there before you made a complete and total ass of yourself. *God!*" he screamed. He banged the heels of his hands on the steering wheel.

"But I was just dancing," I said, my voice a child's. Weren't we all having fun? This was my first party, sure, but I was taking cues from the other kids. It wasn't like I was out there dancing alone. But Clay made it clear that I'd just gone to my first high school party and made a complete mockery of myself.

"Girls can't dance at parties like that, Julie. You basically just told all those guys that you are ready and willing to have sex with every single one of them. You're lucky I got you out of there." Slowly, tears came and I put my face in my hands. It was then, finally, that he started the car and squealed out into the street.

I wept quietly the whole way home. He didn't speak. Just clenched his teeth and writhed his hands around the steering wheel. When we pulled up to the house, I went straight into my room and quietly closed the door. I climbed into bed. I didn't take off my clothes, just kicked off my penny loafers and slipped under the flowered sheets.

I had shamed and embarrassed myself, and I understood the gravity of what I'd done. In bed, I planned my penance. I would never dance at a party again. I would decline invitations to parties. *Remember this*, I told myself. *Remember this awful feeling.* I tried to imprint in my mind that the best decision would always be to stay home, stay safe, and spend the night alone. I became known as the runner, the athlete who was always training, could never really party, who rarely went out, and always had everything under control.

BOTTOM

LATE MAY 1996

It had been three weeks since the fishing trip, where I'd seen that small but bright flicker of happiness. Within a few days of returning to Ohio, the light had extinguished entirely. I was home. Dad was back at work, preparing for another very stressful bet-the-company trial. If my dad succeeded at his legal argument, the company would survive and hundreds of people would keep their jobs. If not, they all faced unemployment and major losses. In my dad's absence, my mom tiptoed around, asking nothing of me. I was the precious vase she didn't disturb for fear that a slight tremor would send me off the shelf and into pieces on the floor. She fed me when I accepted food, but otherwise we merely coexisted. There was a sour fog of failure around me; I felt it. I could almost smell it.

My brother was living about five miles away in an apartment with two other guys. He had a fiancée named Megan now, was madly in love, and couldn't wait to start living with her. I don't remember Clay coming home that summer. It is very likely that he did see me in my malaise, but I don't remember. Perhaps the sight of him shut me down? Perhaps I was too embarrassed about my condition to leave my room and say hello? Or, most likely, we saw each other and I acted as if everything was fine. The part of me that craved the instantly gratifying ease of denial loved pretending things were fine, while the part of me trapped in childhood trauma raged silently beneath my quiet exterior.

Those long, dark weeks, I stayed on the couch, sometimes watching television, but mostly sleeping and then waking and staring at the couch's back cushion. It was maroon, a wide stitch, full of bodily smells from years of evening escape into the television. Day after day I would wake up, walk from my bedroom to the couch, fall asleep, wake up, stare at the couch cushion, maybe weep or think about going to the bathroom before drifting back to sleep. The pattern quickly became irresistible.

It was late spring. The weather was warm and bright, and I lay inside completely inert. I hoped to die. I hoped for a heart attack that would send me to the hospital where nurses would tend to me with care and ask me what was wrong. What I felt was more than sadness. It had become an irresistible blackness. I began to love falling into that dark place. I clung to the awful feelings because they were so familiar, so honest, so intoxicating, and they shut out everything else. There was no room for considering that I could try again at life, that I could try even though I might fail, that someday I could feel better. I fantasized about dying, then sat frozen with fear that I would indeed someday cease to live.

"Do you want something to eat?" my mom would whisper, rubbing my back gently.

"No," I'd mumble.

"Do you want to come with me to the store?"

"No."

"Okay, well, I'll be back in about half an hour," she'd say, a slight exasperation in her voice.

The days like this became endless, merged into one long, bleak existence. I had never experienced this kind of gravity. The thought of getting up and going somewhere, doing something, exhausted me. So I didn't do a thing. For days. My mom's school year had ended, and she was home with me each day, but that made no difference. My favorite place was officially the dark crease between the cushions on the back of the couch. My face felt best pushed deep into that crack. Sensory deprivation had become the only way to comfort myself. I needed to be alone with no light, no sounds, no smells, and as little air circulation as possible. The breeze from an opened door hurt my skin.

I don't know how many days I spent like this. Five? Ten? But finally, one afternoon, my dad came home from work at about two in the afternoon. Maybe my mom had called him in desperation. Maybe he'd seen me there on the couch for too many days and the sight made him unable to focus at his desk.

When he walked into the family room at around two on that average afternoon, there was no noise, just me trying to keep breathing. He walked over to me and said, "Julie?" I didn't have the energy to respond. "You've got to get up," he said.

Eventually I replied with a muffled, "No."

"Yes," he said. "Come on."

"I can't," I mumbled. I started crying.

"Yes, you can," he said, putting his hand on my back. I pushed my face into the cushion and sobbed. My hair was a matted, tangled mess. I could feel the clump of hair shift as I shook my head no. I wanted him to leave; I wanted him to never leave.

I felt his hands push under my body, and he began to pick me up.

"No, no, no, no," I wept. I didn't want to be carried anywhere. I could only exist there on that couch. That was my only place left.

"We are going outside. You need to get outside," he said.

"I can't," I said in a whimper. "Dad, I can't."

"I'll help you," he said, quietly. "I'm here, and I'll help you." I put my arms around him and buried my face in his neck, his smell encoded in me, cologne and skin and father. "Dear, get the door," he said. I heard my mom's slippers rush to the front door, and he carried me down our front step and onto the driveway. "Can you stand?" he asked. I couldn't imagine letting go of him. I believed that there was no way I could actually stand up, especially outside. But I felt him letting my legs go, and I put one foot on the ground, then the other. He held me on our driveway, said to my mom who was watching, "It's okay, honey. I've got it." She went inside and closed the door gently. This was a moment for only my father to witness. It was as if he dipped his arm down into the burning depths of hell and would let it burn if only I would please, please take hold of his hand.

"We're just going to go for a little walk, okay?" he said, in a voice that was easy-going. Simple. A *you can do this* voice. He was still wearing his suit pants and a red tie. He'd loosened his collar a bit and rolled up his sleeves. "Just a little stroll," he whispered, like a meditation. "Just down our driveway, to the next driveway, then we'll turn around. You talk if you're ready. You tell me what you need. Tell me anything."

I leaned on him heavily and he held me with his strong arms. I focused on his strawberry-blond arm hair as we walked. He'd been a redhead as a child; I'd been born with red hair. We were kindred spirits. I wanted to be more of a priority in his life. I didn't feel worthy. I felt terrible at this very moment for making him miss work to tend to stupid, worthless me.

We made it to the end of our driveway, my feet moving mindlessly beneath me. I used to sprint down these roads, my legs so strong and my future so full of promise. Now here I was, feeling lucky that I'd walked 300 feet.

The air outside lifted me just an ounce, made me remember I could move again. It felt miraculous that just walking down our long driveway took some of the blackness away. As we reached our neighbor's driveway and turned around, I finally opened my eyes and squinted in the sunlight.

"I don't know what's wrong with me, Dad," I said.

"It's okay," he said. "You'll be okay."

"I don't know if I will," I said, weeping now. "I really don't."

"You're still you," he said. "You're still beautiful and smart and strong."

I couldn't talk anymore, just nodded and wiped the tears

streaming down my cheeks. He granted me a merciful silence, just held my waist tightly as we walked, like I'd been in a car accident and these were my first steps since the bones had healed. I closed my eyes and let him guide me back up the driveway. He asked if I wanted some dinner. I said I was too tired. He took me to my bedroom, put me in my bed, slipped off my shoes, and pulled up the sheets. "I'm proud of you, princess," he said. "You did good. I love you."

I closed my eyes, exhausted by the walk, ready for a solid night of sleep. But I felt a bit different, like the blanket of sorrow had transformed from lead to wood.

They say that people don't choose their dogs—dogs choose their people. I like to imagine that at this point, Bunker knew to wait for me. Other families had come to the farm and taken away his three sisters and one brother. Each time new people arrived, he gave them a thorough sniff, concluding that they were not the one he was waiting for. Then he proceeded to ignore them or run away when they bent down to pet him, maybe even lift his leg to pee on one man's nice leather shoe. I like to think that when I was at the bottom, Bunker was fighting to make sure he found me.

Telling Brother

Summer 1994

The summer before my senior year in college, before New York, I worked as a hostess at a restaurant near Ohio State. For a month or two, I lived in my own apartment, but I moved back home the morning after someone was shot on the sidewalk in front of my one-story building.

Being home wore on me. One day, when the feelings took over, I took a knife from the butcher block, ran to the basement and pressed the blade into my skin until I felt pain. That same day, my mother made me come to a birthday dinner for Clay at a fancy restaurant. She was scared to leave me alone, so I was forced to sit, looking disheveled, with Clay and his latest girlfriend as my dad and brother made jokes that struck me as wildly sexist and rude. On the way home from that restaurant, I tried to jump out of my dad's car while he sped along the freeway at 70 miles an hour.

The next day, my mother made my first-ever appointment with a therapist. I went with curious reluctance to her office, sat down in a depressing brown room and heard, for the first time, a professional say, "Your parents tell me that they're worried about you. Can you imagine why that might be?" I explained my circumstances, then couldn't stand listening to the therapist say in a sickly sweet tone, "An older brother is supposed to protect his younger sister. He's supposed to help her, teach her, be kind to her."

"On TV, maybe," I scoffed. "Whatever. All siblings fight."

"Yes, but not like this, they don't. Not like this," her tone shifted and I wondered if I'd exaggerated the stories.

"Julie, you have every right to tell your brother that what he's done to you has affected you."

"Sure, but you don't know what he'll do if I confront him," I said.

"Do you mean that he'll harm you if you bring up the fact that he hurt you both physically and emotionally when you were a young child?" Her nostrils flared in outrage.

"No. No," I said, laughing a little. This was getting ridiculous.

"I doubt he realizes how his treatment affected you," she said. "He needs to know, for his own sake."

"Why?" I asked.

"He's got to know how you feel, that he hurt you, that his treatment was intolerable. That he can't go around treating people with such disregard."

"I would never say that to him," I said. "Intolerable. He would laugh in my face. Besides, he's not awful to everyone. Just me."

"Julie, you need to remember this: His treatment of you has nothing to do with you," she said, so sure of herself.

What? It had everything to do with me. He really hated me, which in turn, made me hate myself. He was my older brother, my role model, the male with whom I spent most of my waking hours. And he hated me. This was what I knew, deeply, at my core. How was I supposed to learn that I was anything other than what he told me? Asking me to stray from the knowledge that he hated me would be like asking a baby born in zero gravity to walk. No matter what inflated praise my father infrequently showered upon me, or how often my mother made me a nice meal, I wanted, above all, for Clay to love me. Instead, he hit me, insulted me, knocked my door down, stepped on my head, argued with me, then pushed me to the ground until I submitted, and this left me dead inside.

Over three sessions, my therapist convinced me to confront him. I rehearsed what I would say. I practiced in the car and in the shower. That weekend, when he stopped home for a visit, I asked him if I could speak to him alone in my bedroom. This itself was unusual. We both acted nonchalant, though we knew this was something we did not do—talk.

I sat on my bed and waited for him to come to my room. He arrived eating chips, a handful cupped to his stomach. "I've been talking with my therapist," I said, shaking slightly, squeezing my flattened, sweaty palms together. "And I want to tell you that the way you treated me over the years has really hurt me and she says it even qualifies as abuse. Like, sibling abuse," I said. Looking back, I don't know what I was expecting him say: *Oh! You're right! I'm so sorry! What an ass I've been!*

I was so caught up in actually getting the words out that I flinched when he started yelling. "Fuck you!" he screamed, potato chips flying from his teeth to my bedspread. He swallowed hard, then hissed, "Jesus Christ, you fucking *bitch*!" He walked toward the door, cursing under his breath, "Holy fucking *Christ*!" I sat with my mouth open mid-word.

What I saw in that moment, in his reaction, felt like a revelation. *He* was hurt. And it wasn't because of anything I said; it was because of something in him. Something made him feel so terrible that he took it out on me. His overly emotional reaction pulled the first veil off of our troubled relationship. I was old enough to see that his hurting me stemmed from his own pain. For a split second, I *was* curious. I was a growing woman examining her hurting older brother. But when he turned around and screamed, "See if I invite you to my fucking wedding!" I was a child again. I nearly fell backwards. We'd never truly fought as adults, except for once when he pushed me to the floor because I thought we should boil our corn on the cob and he thought we should grill it. But now I'd been banished from his future, theoretical wedding. I'd been punished with exile.

He left the room, continuing to curse and mutter down the hallway, and I sat quietly in my room, watching out the window. I heard him slam the front door and drive away. My mom padded down to my bedroom. "What on earth happened?"

"Nothing," I said.

"Sheesh," she said, shaking her head and walking back to the kitchen.

I instantly hated the therapist and decided to stop seeing her—summer was almost over anyway. I lay on my bed wondering if he really would exclude me from his wedding. Could he do that? No. My parents wouldn't let him. I berated myself for my stupidity, thankful that the next week I was due to leave home and go back to college. I couldn't get out of my house fast enough, and spent the next few days packing my room, meticulously cleaning it, as if I were leaving and never, ever coming back.

DOCTOR OF PSYCHIATRY

MAY 1996

The morning after I walked down the driveway with my father, my parents asked me to see a psychiatrist. I said I would, but added that no doctor or therapist had ever helped before. What made them think this would be any different? "This woman is an MD," my dad said, "and she comes very highly recommended by Jon at the firm whose daughter is anorexic." I wondered about my father's life at his law firm. Were they a more satisfying family than us? Did he sit in their offices and talk about his troubles because he could never really relate to any of us at home?

"I wish I was anorexic," I said. "At least I'd be fucked up and thin."

"You don't mean that, Julie," my mom said.

"Whatever," I mumbled.

"You have an appointment tomorrow at 10," my dad said. "Here's the address." He handed me a yellow piece of paper with an address scribbled in his bubbly cursive. The fact that my father had participated in the acquisition of my health care meant that the situation had officially turned dire. A numbness came over me. My ears buzzed. I closed my eyes.

"Okay?" he asked, taking my knee and jiggling it.

"Fine," I said.

My mom glanced at my dad with relief, and he crossed his arms and watched me as if I were a puzzle he had yet to solve.

The next morning I looked forward to the appointment with the shrink. I didn't shower before going, just pulled on black pants, a black shirt, and my steel-toed boots and got in the car. I drove to the building, a glossy, black-windowed office tower in a characterless suburban office park. I sat for a moment after killing the engine, preparing myself. I felt like a boxer entering a ring. This lady had no idea what was about to hit her. I skipped the elevator, took the echoing stairs, and checked in at the yellow Formica front desk.

I flipped through a *National Geographic*, stealing glances at all the other crazies in the waiting room. There was an obese woman with buzzed hair minus a thin braid that she kept about three feet long. She fiddled with the braid and stared at the wall.

"Julie?" a voice said. I stood up and smiled instinctively, then remembered that I had promised myself not to fake anything. I had to be honest this day. My life depended on it.

The psychiatrist wasn't what I expected. She looked like someone's mom. She had short brown hair and was wearing a long denim skirt with a gray and white flowered turtleneck. Her desk was flanked by four tall gray filing cabinets, everything except the computer stacked messily with papers. I flopped down on the black leather couch and stared at the back of her head as she wrote something on a clipboard. She swiveled around to face me.

"Hi," she glanced at the clipboard, "Julie. I'm Dr. Miller. I understand your parents are very concerned about you. Can you tell me why that might be?"

I had to stifle laughter. She was so earnest. So ridiculously fake. She didn't care about me. She didn't *know* me. This was her job. Then, I thought, *I can't take this anymore*, and I felt the tears coming.

"Good luck fixing me," I said, staring at the floor, failing to fight the tears that betrayed my attempt at a steely exterior. "I've been to about ten therapists and no one has been able to help."

"Well, I'm not a therapist," she said. "I'm a psychiatrist. I'm an M.D. I can help you figure out if there's something wrong physiologically that we might be able to help you with."

My cheeks flushed. *Fuck.* This was bad. I'd been sent to the crazy doctor. Maybe this had all gone too far. Surely I could snap out of it. Shame fluttered through me, and the tears came hard.

"Can you tell me why you're crying?" Dr. Miller said in a quiet voice.

"Because I always fucking cry," I said. "It's my thing."

"Okay, can you tell me what you're feeling right now?"

I wanted to tell her that I was terrified, that I didn't want to go to an institution, or that maybe I did. I just couldn't fathom feeling better, and I didn't know if I wanted to feel better anymore.

Instead I told her about Clay, about my dad working all the time and my mom always being *fine* and never really talking to me. I told her about losing my boyfriend and leaving my job in New York and not knowing what I was going to do with my life. I told her about hating Ohio, about hating myself, about sleeping and eating sugar to dull the pain, about having no friends left.

"Do you ever think about suicide?" she asked. We made eye contact. I knew enough about doctors to know that you never tell them you're thinking about suicide if you really are.

"Not really," I said. "Just being really injured. I want someone in a hospital to take care of me. I want to be broken so I can be fixed."

"Okay," she said, like we were done. She swiveled back to her desk. I checked the clock. We'd been talking for forty-four minutes. She handed me a piece of paper and said, "Take this to the front desk and they'll get you all set up."

"Set up with what?" I asked, thinking they were going to wrap me in a straitjacket and toss me down the old laundry chute reserved for the too-far-gone cases.

"Just a follow-up appointment with a new therapist, and maybe some medication," she said. "Thanks so much for agreeing to come. You did the right thing." She gave me a tight smile before looking back down at her paperwork. I stepped into the hallway and she closed the door behind me. I stared at a faded picture in a flimsy silver frame on the wall, an eagle soaring over pine trees. Then I read the paper in my hands. She'd circled, "Major Depression—MD—First Episode."

I wanted to collapse and cheer. I'd been given a checkbox for a fucking psychiatric disorder. There was a reason that this was happening, but holy shit, I was sick-in-the-head! I had never known anyone who had been diagnosed with depression. In my quick estimation, this was shameful and scary. I felt swept away by this piece of paper, and there was not a bone in my body that thought for a moment that the psychiatrist might be wrong. I took a deep breath to let it soak in. Then, as was my habit, I placed this diagnosis right next to all the other diagnoses I'd absorbed over the years. Ugly, Weird, Stupid, Fat, Unlikable, please meet your newest teammate: Depressed.

Pale Yellow Pills

May 1996

I sat on my living room floor in front of the television. Pamphlets and stapled stacks of paper surrounded me. My parents were trying to look busy in the kitchen while sneaking glances as I read about these drugs they wanted me to swallow, these drugs that would change my brain. Because something was terribly wrong with my brain. All of this felt like a kick to the gut.

The picture on the front of the Zoloft pamphlet showed a sunrise under bright blue, italicized block letters. The blue-jean-dress psychiatrist had given me a prescription for this medication, and I left her office convinced I would never take such a drug. The thought of swallowing medication that would affect my brain seemed ludicrous. Why would I ever do such a thing?

Still, as I drove home from her office, down the central Ohio roads cradled under huge trees with brilliant green leaves, I felt a shift. This dark, scary, oh-so-phenomenal pain I was suffering might be treatable by a drug. If they'd made a drug for the awful way I felt, then this was something others had felt before too. That thought alone pulled me one smidge out of the blackness. There were others like me. But where? Were they all hiding on their parents' couches too? Why didn't anyone ever talk to me about feeling down? *Really* down? Was this so shameful that it shouldn't be discussed aloud?

After my flat-out refusal to take the drug, my parents went into research mode. My dad found and printed every piece of data he could about depression and selective serotonin reuptake inhibitors (SSRIs). He brought them home and handed them to me. "Just read it and see what you think," he said. "You don't have to do anything."

Part of me wanted to remain this way—fucked up and sad—to show my poor, gallant, hopeful, caring father that some things weren't fixable, especially people. Or to punish him, to expose that I was broken partly because of his absences. But those truths were beginning to be overrun by the bit of me that wanted to feel happiness: genuine, deep, inside-out happiness. I wondered if I could be happy; I honestly didn't know. I didn't know how being okay and staying okay felt. The thought was enticing enough that I continued reading the Zoloft pamphlets.

I read about side effects, hoping for weight loss and skin improvements, but instead found weight gain and loss of libido. Then I read what this drug helped eliminate: prolonged feelings of sadness, hopelessness, and worthlessness, sometimes running in the family, sometimes not. The pamphlets described an inability to function that was sometimes triggered by traumatic events such as breakups or moves, and childhood events such as abuse and neglect. This was *me*. Had my parents forged this? Had my dad hired a doctor friend to write this just for my convincing?

After an hour of leafing through the pages, I landed at the final conclusion: Why not? It couldn't get much worse. I gathered the pile of documentation that Sunday morning and walked into the dining room where my parents were reading the newspaper. I stood before them, their faces open and hopeful. "Okay," I said.

"Okay what?" my mom said.

"Okay, she'll take the medication," my dad said, smiling at me. My mom's eyes searched mine, wanting confirmation that he was right.

"Sure," I said. "Why the fuck not? It's just my brain."

"Julie," my mom chided.

"Fuck it. It can't get much worse," I said, noticing a hummingbird hovering outside at a yellow and red feeder. My parents, in their silence, agreed.

Within the hour, my mom drove the prescription to the drug store. My dad and I sat and watched a football game on television while we waited for the pills to come.

"Want anything?" my dad asked before he went to the kitchen for a handful of cookies and a soda.

"Nope, I'm fine," I said, acutely aware of how far from fine I was. The decision to take the pills terrified me. I was sick, really sick. I sat on the couch huddled in a ball and fell asleep without noticing.

When my mom came back from the store, I woke up and went to the kitchen. She handed me the pills and we stood on opposite sides of the kitchen's island.

"You know what else might help me?" I said. Her face brightened like I'd just told her we'd won ten million dollars while she was at the drug store. The fact that I had a potential solution for my terrible malaise appeared astonishing to her.

"A puppy," I said. I could hardly believe I'd said it. I was sure my mother would laugh at the idea, but she didn't laugh or scoff or sigh. She knew me well enough to know that this wasn't a joke or a dark stab at a stupid solution. "One that's mine," I said.

"I think that's a great idea." Her face relaxed. Then her tone shifted into skepticism. "I'm not sure what Cinder will think, but that's okay." She offered a nervous laugh. Her ever-so-slight negative reaction to my very first attempt at self-help bristled deeply. Didn't she know how hard I was trying?

"She'll be fine," I said, starting to walk away, knowing I was being an asshole but too hurt and sensitive to help myself.

"What kind do you want?" my mom asked as I left the kitchen, then, "Great idea, honey!" she said, just before I slammed my bedroom door.

Here we were again. My mother said something innocent that cut me sideways, and I couldn't stop the rage. I couldn't stop wanting to punish her when all she was trying to do was love me in the best way she knew how.

I'd been taking the medication for seven days but still didn't feel different. Mornings were tough; waking up was the hardest. I would lie in bed for an hour or more after my body awoke. Physically getting up felt too emotionally difficult. My parents' mantra had become *Two weeks*. Two weeks until the medication kicks in. They were desperately hoping the Zoloft would help lift me out of the darkness.

We'd talked about getting the dog soon, and over oatmeal that Sunday, without asking her to, my mom perused the classifieds looking for puppies. She held a steaming cup of coffee in her hand as she read aloud, "Australian shepherds six weeks AKC, Beagle puppies, German shepherd..." She was scanning down the page to golden retrievers. I'd gone to the bookstore and bought two books: *Prozac Nation* and *A Guide to Your Purebred Puppy*. I tore through *Prozac Nation*, a little frightened by Elizabeth Wurtzel's too familiar, dark and self-destructive reaction to feeling the same way I did. When I needed a break from the Wurtzel book, I perused the puppy book. Each breed was ranked according to traits like the amount of exercise required, the ease of training, and sociability with strangers. I earmarked about eight breeds in the sporting group: Brittany spaniels, golden and flat-coated retrievers, Labrador retrievers, Irish setters, Weimaraner and English springer spaniels. I studied each page with surprising focus and found myself returning to golden retrievers: easy to train, loyal, big, great running partners, and beautiful. A family dog. My new family.

I also bought a book on training and was reading about how to bring a dog home so that the transition was as smooth and trauma-free as possible. I bought a crate, food bowls, and a leash. The preparation was a welcome distraction.

"Golden retriever, AKC pups, ready to go," my mom pointed at the newspaper with her cherry-red fingernail. I had to grin as she put down her coffee, snatched up a purple pen, and circled the ad. "Here's another one. Golden Pups, Parents on Site, City of Alexandria." She circled that one too and wrote down both phone numbers. I was learning to recognize that my mother's willingness to help me get things done was the way she tried to connect with me. This was how she knew to express herself: with actions, not words. I hadn't apologized for my rudeness the other night. I never apologized to my mother; she rarely asked it of me; and still, she showed up. I imagine now that I would have imploded much earlier had she punished me or been angry about my awful behavior. These are things I didn't consider then. I couldn't fathom not having my mother with me, on my side, always forgiving me until I finally figured out that inflicting pain on her was not actually what I wanted to do. How very lucky I was.

She called two of the phone numbers, and they confirmed that we could come see the puppies that day. We dressed quickly, jumped into her top-down red convertible and pulled out of the driveway. It was a blissful mid-summer day in central Ohio: seventy degrees, bright sun, and puffy clouds. Flowers bloomed everywhere. The summer bugs were just beginning their daily chorus.

I'd begun seeing a new therapist named Mya. She was young—a therapist in training. She was under thirty years old, had just moved to Ohio from Seattle, and I liked her immediately. Her soft-spoken tenderness put me at ease. She was pretty with straight brown hair and striking green eyes. She crossed her legs at her ankles and wore solid colored skirts that ended just below her knee. I told her about wanting a puppy and she said she thought that sounded like a perfect idea.

My mom drove us down our street and turned onto the long two-lane road that would eventually lead us to the highway. We didn't talk. I leaned back in the seat, holding an old towel. The book said that the best place for a puppy to ride home was on a towel in his new owner's lap. I couldn't imagine a wiggly puppy wanting to sit in my lap in a convertible. Maybe we'd have to put the top up.

The first litter we saw was at a house in the suburbs east of Columbus. We walked up onto the front porch and a friendly middle-aged woman came outside, pointing us to the walkway around the side of the house.

"They're all back here," she said, wiping her palms on a soiled apron with faded pink flowers. "We have two of them sold already, but two are still available. Both females." We opened a chain link gate and saw a six-foot-wide wire pen in the center of a big grassy lawn. The flimsy metal practically burst with the excitement from the puppies.

They were irresistible: fuzzy white blond fur, eager sparkly brown eyes, and big floppy paws. The woman's three children also came out to the yard, and they showed us that it was okay to reach in and pick up a puppy, let it run in the grass. Each puppy barked and squirmed, jumping in an effort to be free. I laughed and picked up a little female. Her razor-sharp puppy teeth grazed my hand as she leapt out of my grasp to go run in the yard. Within a minute, she was in a full sprint, racing to catch up with her siblings. She stumbled and landed chin first in the grass, her little tail flailing. She regained her footing, sat up, shook her head, and took off again. We watched them play, happy in their freedom, but the pups didn't come back to us. They played in the yard, oblivious to our voices. I went over to them, tried to call one to me. I'd read in the book that when you're choosing a puppy, the puppies that wander off and don't look back are likely to do that when they're grown up as well. I turned to my mom who stood smiling with her arms crossed.

"Let's go look at the other litter," I whispered.

"Okay," she nodded. She turned to the woman and said, "Thank you so much for showing us your beautiful puppies. We'll let you know if we decide one of them is right for us." I was so impressed with how my mom said her polite no-thank-you. I nodded in an awkward way that was supposed to convey, *Thanks* and *Sorry.* Neither sentiment translated and the lady gestured in a way that said: *I'm not insulted. Should I be insulted?* I felt overwhelmed. I hated people. I wanted to go home and hide on the couch.

We got back in the car and drove farther east past the Franklin County line, way out into the countryside toward the little hamlet of Alexandria. A few trees lined the roads, and beyond them stretched endless fields: soy, corn, wheat, and potatoes all the way to the horizon. These fields calmed me with their simplicity, their singular purpose. We drove down near-empty country roads that every once in a while intersected another two-lane road. We'd stop, look around, then continue on our way. Birds perched idle on telephone wires, some taking off with the approaching rush of our engine, their wings pulling them up higher, higher, and away.

I closed my eyes, breathed deep. These were just like the roads I ran on during my last semester of my senior year in college. My classes were over by 2 p.m., so every day at two thirty I strapped on my running shoes and left campus. The only promise I made to myself was that I would jog slowly, take a different route every day, look up at the trees and sky when I ran, and only skip one day a week. It was the beginning of a few of the happiest, most peaceful months of my life. In New York, I would walk down shadowy sidewalks dreaming of the openness of central Ohio, yearning for roads flanked by fields, for their freedom and isolation. These roads cradled me. I realized this now. I'd been trying to hate Ohio, because it was so hard to be at home. But the land had actually always been there for me all along. As a child, the moon had lit my room on sad nights. I'd wandered cornfields and puttered around at Lehman's Pond. Those were some of my best childhood memories. And here we were, my mother and I, only thirty or so miles south of my college, sailing along a quiet country road after my breakdown, on the search for my new family. I comprehended at that moment that I was beginning to actively try to heal.

As we neared the farm, I closed my eyes and took a deep breath, letting my head fall back so that the sun warmed my pale face. I accepted that lovely moment with gratitude and hope.

When I felt the car turn, I squinted and saw a long gravel driveway flanked on either side by fields that had gone to seed with weeds and wildflowers. At the end of the driveway stood a tall white farmhouse cradled by a crescent of century-old trees. Dogs barked as our tires crunched up the drive. A lanky red golden retriever ran toward our car, tail wagging, barking, hackles raised. A few puppies ran in the yard behind the house, free of fences. This was looking good so far.

A tall blonde woman in her fifties stepped out of the farmhouse's side door, the screen door slapping shut behind her. She waved and smiled at us as we cut the engine and stepped out of the car. "Ooh! A convertible!" she said. "Great day for it." My mom smiled and introduced herself. We all shook hands.

"Well, here they are," she said. There were no puppies that I could see. She winked and stuck two fingers in her mouth, belting out a window-shattering whistle. From around the house and out of the woods emerged three little orange puppies and one adult golden. The breeder told us that she'd already housebroken the puppies and trained them to come when called. The larger dogs were almost as red as Blarney, a maroon, Irish setter red. They romped up to her and she praised them, "Oh, you good little guys. How smart you are." The puppies jumped on her and she kneed them off. It seemed harsh to me, but they didn't seem to care. They rolled in the grass then righted themselves, eagerly sniffing the ground, peeing on tall weeds.

"You don't have a fence for them?" my mom asked. I bristled at her question. I loved that these dogs were roaming free. Their first taste of the world was one of freedom, not being caged.

"Well, you know," the woman said, "I was second-guessing this approach last week when all the dogs went missing and I had to hike down to Raccoon Creek just before dark and fish them all out of the water." She laughed and bent over, grabbing one of the puppies and holding him in her arms until he squirmed away. "We crate them at night. Little rascals," she said.

My mom, still concerned, began asking her about Raccoon Creek, how far it was, and if the dogs had to cross any major roads before getting there. I dropped out of the conversation and wandered over to the dirt yard where the puppies were playing. One of the older dogs spotted me, came over and pressed her dark-red shoulder into my thigh. I bent down, put my face into her neck and inhaled. She smelled like soil and mint. "Hi," I whispered. She stayed still, panting, appearing pleased.

I stood up, watching the puppies. How would I ever choose? The chapter on how to choose the right puppy said there was the cradle test, the sound-sensitivity test, the touch-sensitivity test. The book said that emotion played a part in choosing a puppy, but that it was important to use knowledge and common sense before turning to emotion. I felt flooded with doubt. What if I chose wrong?

As I fretted, I noticed that one of the puppies had spotted me from the edge of the woods. He walked over toward me, then paused, still watching me, before coming closer and sitting down at my feet. He looked up into my eyes, his own mud-brown eyes nestled under expressive little eyebrow nubs, his tiny chin hairs glowing in the light, his orange-red paws caked with mud. In that moment, of course, I knew. There he was. I hadn't been forced to choose; I'd been chosen. I picked him up and he licked my nose. He smelled like dirt and metal and wet dog. My dog had found me.

"This one," I said, turning to my mom and the breeder. They were still chatting and didn't hear me. I walked closer to them. "This is the one," I said. I was sure, and that surge of confidence came as a jolt. It had been so long since I'd felt sure of anything. The puppy sat calmly in my arms, not squirming one bit, trusting me to hold the full weight of his body.

"Great!" my mom said. She looked at the breeder as if to ask if this was okay. The breeder paused, looking confused, like maybe this puppy wasn't actually available. Had they decided that this was the one they wanted to keep? In that split second, I was planning my getaway, which, were it to fail, gave way to an elaborate plan for a dark-of-night theft.

"Oh, him," she said. She put a finger on her lips. "What color is his collar?" I looked down.

"Green," I said.

"Oh, yes. Good. Sure. Of course. He's yours!" She laughed. "He looks just like his brother that we're keeping. Thank goodness for color coding!" I laughed too, trying to hide my immense relief.

He stayed in my arms while my mom wrote the check. I was aware that my mom was buying this dog for me, and made a mental note to pay her back as soon as I had another job. I let him back down on the ground to say good-bye to his parents and siblings, but he came back to me and looked up at me again. He seemed to want me, not them. It was hard to comprehend, but our meeting felt something like two magnets clacking together, two universes colliding, two hands clasping. I was absolutely sure that this was my dog and that I was meant to find him. Of course, I felt this groundswell of confidence, then immediately questioned it, nearly dismissing it. After all, it was official: I wasn't right in the head.

I carried him over to his mother, put him down next to her and he twirled in the dirt, chasing his tail or maybe it was a fly. His mama stood still, confident, sniffing something that seemed distant, a faraway scent carried on the breeze. Her eyes were half closed and glistening, her red feathers hung long, only the end of her tail wagged back and forth. I petted her gently down her rib cage, kissed her soft head, and whispered, "Thank you, mama." She opened her mouth, panting, letting her tongue dangle to the side before trotting off toward the trees.

I called the puppy back to me with a click of my tongue and he ran straight to me. The giddy charge of a dog responding to me, coming to me when I called, left me nearly dizzy with bliss.

We said good-bye to the breeder and I held the puppy close to my chest. "Thank you, Mom," I said, "for paying for him." I couldn't adequately express my gratitude. She watched me, pausing, probably because I actually appeared happy. It was as if the moment I picked him up, *I* felt lifted. Already I couldn't fathom the thought of ever letting him go. I felt a perceptible shift the moment I met him. A reuniting. A lifting. A glimpse of hope.

Bunker Hill

Afternoon, June 26, 1996

I didn't use the towel; I just let the puppy lie in my lap. He showed no signs of distress or fear. He seemed content in our car, as if he considered this as good a place as any.

His head was small, like the size of an apple. His fur was mottled red, dull and matte but soft as down. The fur didn't sit down yet—it stood up, poked out—making him look mildly electrically shocked. He glanced at me, his eyes nearly bloodshot with what appeared to be fatigue. As we drove away from the farm, it seemed that the motion of the car or the warmth of my lap helped him remember that he was desperately, urgently tired. He was asleep within seconds, the full weight of him falling into me.

I felt like crying, but this time, joyful tears. This beautiful, innocent little creature was mine, and he trusted me already. His warmth on my lap grounded me in a way I needed. I could feel myself pulling back to the earth, like a kite reeled in during a storm. It was the strangest moment, and I didn't trust it. Surely within the hour, the sadness would return and load me with guilt for taking on such an enormous responsibility in my fragile mental state.

I took his right paw and snuck in a sensitivity test, gently pinching in between his toes. According to the book, if he were to react, I might be in for a wild ride with an easily agitated pup. He didn't flinch. Instead, he pushed his head into my abdomen, letting his big left paw drop down onto my thigh, as if he were offering a one-legged hug.

His back was curled with his hind paws stretched, nearly

touching his nose. I studied his ribs, dragging two fingers lightly down either side of his spine. We were on the freeway now, but I barely noticed. His dirty brown nose flared as he slept, as if he was cataloguing smells even while asleep. I watched him and fell completely, irretrievably, head-over-heels in love.

Then I began to panic. Less than ten miles from the farm, the thoughts crept in. I had no income. I lived with my parents. I had no idea what I was going to do with my life. I didn't know what city I would move to next, where I would live, or whether I could manage life with a dog. What the hell was I doing adopting a puppy? I couldn't stop the thoughts. Then I put my hands on the puppy, stroked his fluffy orange fur, felt his velvety ears, and it was as if the thoughts were diffused bombs. The blackness fizzled when I touched this dog, and in their place appeared a quiet calm.

"He's beautiful, Julie," my mom said, watching him snooze in my lap. She put her eyes back on the road, pushed her hair behind her ear, and smiled as she drove. The light was hitting her brown hair so that it shone almost golden, and I felt such gratitude for her get-it-done nature. She couldn't talk to me about what was happening, but she knew me well enough to know what might help— even something as major as accepting a pooping, peeing, barking, chewing animal into her beautifully appointed home.

Forty-five minutes later, we pulled up to the house and the puppy's eyes opened when the car turned off. "Hi, baby," I said in a gentle voice. I had an instant agenda. I wanted this dog to know he was safe with me. I wanted him to know that we had lucked out in finding each other, that I would do my best to give him a good life. I had a huge responsibility that I knew I could fulfill. I could *do* this. I could do it well. This confidence felt astonishing.

"What are you going to name him?" my mom asked as she stepped out of the car.

"I don't know," I said slowly, smiling at her. I held his cheek to mine, taking in his dirty-puppy smell. His tail wagged. "I love him. I just love him."

I took him to our back yard where he walked around, sniffed, peed, and burst out with a spontaneous fit of running in circles, racing to me, then dodging me at the last minute. I was laughing. A few weeks from the day my dad forced me to walk down the driveway, I was sitting outside in the grass, laughing with a little red puppy. He was so full of life and joy. I'd begun taking the medication a week before, and though I couldn't feel a difference yet, perhaps this hope hinted at some kind of change.

My mom let Cinder outside. She was eleven now, and not at all amused at the sight of a puppy in her yard. The puppy lunged toward her and she cowered, then turned and trotted back inside through the doggie door. We laughed as the puppy watched the house with great interest, as if wondering how on earth the old black dog had disappeared into a wall.

"What about Max?" I said. "Does he look like a Max?"

"Sure," my mom said.

"No, he needs something meaningful. What about Sundance? Sunny for short?"

"I don't know if he looks like a Sunny," my mom said.

"What was your first dog's name?" I asked.

"Well, let's see. That was Bunker Hill. The beagle."

"What happened to him?" I asked.

"Oh," she said. "He was hit by a car. He was the *best* dog. We had him in law school. He was Cornell Law School Class of 1970's unofficial mascot."

"Bunker Hill," I said. I watched as the puppy stepped on the end of a stick then startled when the other end popped up. Again, I laughed. The sound of my own laughter struck me as beautiful, a thought I'd never had. Then this thought: *Don't get egotistical. You're so full of yourself.*

After a while, I said, "I think that's it. Bunker Hill. Bunker. Bunker!" I called in a high voice. I patted the grass with my hands. He trotted over to me, his tongue hanging out the side of his mouth. He sat down at my feet.

"Did you see that?" I asked my mom.

"I think he likes that name," she said.

I nodded and my mom told me she was going inside to get some laundry done. I turned back to my puppy. "Bunker Hill," I said, aloud. "Bunker. Bunk." I liked the name, and I loved that it paid homage to my mom and dad, to the beginning of their lives together. Creating such a tradition imbued a wild hope in me. In the last few months, my parents had saved my life. My mom hadn't told me to stop crying and pull it together when I called disoriented and sobbing from New York. My dad *wanted* to understand. He wanted to know what was wrong and how he could help. They believed me when I told them how acutely I was suffering, and they rescued me when I was, conceivably, old enough to rescue myself. Naming this puppy Bunker felt like a way of communicating that I felt forever indebted to their patience, forgiveness, and devotion.

I had a feeling that the name could also be an homage to the battle I was fighting within. So I went to the living room and pulled out our encyclopedia, the thirty-volume tome to which I'd referred countlessly throughout my primary school years, its edges bound with crinkly gold. The "B" volume said that the Battle of Bunker Hill was an epic clash fought during the Revolutionary War in which the Colonials lost to the British, but the British suffered 800 wounded soldiers and over 200 dead. The still meager colonial forces began to hope that, despite the loss, they might actually be able to someday defeat their overwhelming enemy. So the colonial forces retreated and regrouped, emerging stronger, more confident. Even though they were small compared to their foe, this battle gave them hope that one day they would prevail. I closed the encyclopedia. *Bunker Hill.* The name was perfect.

We went back outside and Bunker ran to me, then plopped down in the grass, pressing his back to my leg. He pushed against me and rolled over. I felt like I'd known him my entire life—like we were twins reunited after being separated at birth. I lay down next to him and looked at the sky, the white clouds sailing by above. The earth beneath me felt cool, wet, soft, regenerative. I put my hand on his chest and he wiggled, then looked at me upside-down with his forehead squished in the grass. I thought of all of those meditative days as a child outside, with the trees and animals and fresh air. And at that moment it occurred to me that perhaps with him by my side, I could try again at independence. I could try another city. I had no idea which one, but I felt optimistic that it could happen. That optimism felt like a miracle.

The moon on June 26, 1996, the day Bunker came into my life, was 68 percent full and waxing. Moment by moment, it grew bigger and brighter. Bunker and I found each other when the moon was half full, the light half returned. We would begin the process of growing and healing together right alongside the moon: brighter each day, little by little.

DAY ONE

JUNE 27, 1996

Bunker's first night was restless. I followed the book's emphatic instruction and locked him in the crate next to my bed for the night. He whined at first but quieted when I lay down next to him. I pushed my hand through the crate's bars to pet him. He licked my fingers, gnawed on them a bit, then circled twice and lay down with a thud.

In the middle of the night, he began to whimper. I pulled myself out of bed and took him outside to pee, craning my neck to study the night sky. The sky in summer darkness pulsed with stars, the chorus of crickets an echoing beat. I was drowsy, but also aware that I was happy at that moment to be awake, to actually witness the sparkling light of stars in all the blackness.

I returned to my room in a sleepy daze. I led Bunker back to the crate and talked to him in a low, soothing voice. "It's okay, buddy. It's okay." He pulled back when he saw the crate, not wanting to re-enter, so I crawled in as far as I could go, my legs still hanging out, and patted the bottom of the crate. He followed me inside, licked my face and sniffed my ears, giving me chills.

Finally he curled up with his warm back against my chest. He took a deep breath and closed his eyes, tucking his nose further into the fluffy towels that lined the crate. It occurred to me as I gently stroked his side that this was the first time in recent memory that *I* was reassuring another living thing. And, miraculously, I knew in that moment that I was more than capable of caring for him. I felt enormously driven to create a space for Bunker that felt safe, free of all worry, fear, and anxiety. For the first time in a long time, I felt as if I had a purpose.

I couldn't imagine treating myself kindly, with gentle understanding. But I could, without question, do that for my dog. Perhaps part of what began to save me was that I started creating this sacred, safe space where he and I met. In this space, there was no ridicule. There was no doubt or loneliness. There was no sorrow or anger. It was just pure, beautiful being. It was us looking at the world with wide-eyed, forever hopeful puppy wonder.

I put my nose near his back, smelled his fur, tried to memorize the curve of his spine, the rise and fall of his breath. After a while, when he was limp with deep sleep, I scooted out, then locked the crate as quietly as I could and fell back into bed, asleep in seconds.

Since leaving New York, I'd slept until noon most days. There was no reason to wake up. Sleep was one of the only ways to dampen the sadness. It was 6:45 a.m. when I heard several high-pitched barks emanating from the crate. I opened my eyes and saw Bunker's face, felt his breath on my cheek. As soon as he saw me stir, he stood up, wagging his tail so hard that the metal crate rocked back and forth, jangling with sound. He poked his nose out of the crate's wires, his eyes locked on mine. I laughed, smiled, and said a slow, sleepy "Hi, Bunk."

I stretched, pointing my toes, which dangled off the too-small twin bed. Every morning of my life, I had woken up longing to sleep more, wanting to disappear. I sat up. The sun shone bright through my bedroom's blinds and I pulled them up slightly to let some of the light flood the room. Then this thought: *I want to get out of bed.*

It struck me that this must be how not-depressed people feel when they wake up: They feel okay, no dread, ready to start the day. It wasn't until the awful waking dread was gone that I realized that it had been there as long as I could remember. The fact that it had lifted meant that there was a chance I could get better.

I opened Bunker's crate and led him outside to the yard,

standing in my bare feet and pajamas, telling him to go potty. When he did, I bent down, praised him, and let him lick my cheek before he ran back into the yard, his paws wet with morning dew. I watched him play, the warm orange summer sun rising, shining through the trunks of the trees. He sniffed a spot, then flipped over to roll in it. I walked over to him to see what he was rolling in— hopefully not a dead rodent. He stood up and sniffed again and I noticed an earthworm writhing above the soil. "You like worms, huh?" I asked, and he flopped down, neck first, on the slimy little creature. I smiled and walked back to the patio.

Out of the corner of my eye, I spotted my mom at the family room window, watching me. Not only was I awake, I was in the back yard laughing and smiling. She didn't wave or acknowledge me, just grinned and turned back into the family room, coffee clutched in her hand.

No Wonder

Early July 1996

At eleven weeks old, Bunker walked like he still hadn't figured out what legs were for. I watched him for hours, laughing much of the time. Watching him took me out of my mind and into the moment as he so adorably tripped over air or tried but failed to catch a housefly. I observed as Bunker listened, deeply, to the forest behind my parents' house. He froze at the sound of a cracking branch, or took off on a scent trail like a released spring, blades of grass tickling his round belly. For him, there was no fretting, no worry. Just this moment. This joy. Maybe, I thought, I should try to be more like him.

I learned to read his expressions. I knew that his ears went back when he was startled. If I wasn't close by, I could see that his eyes widened almost imperceptibly, then darted until they found me. The feeling was mutual. When he saw me, his body curled like an apostrophe in happiness and I knew—he liked me. My confidence in my own likability had always been so shaky. But I knew Bunker had no reason to fool me, no reason to lie or pass judgment. The shedding of that layer of doubt left me feeling so light I imagined I might float right up into the highest branches of the trees and spend the day there.

Out in the yard one afternoon, when I was failing to teach Bunker to fetch, he stopped mid-stride, pointed his muzzle straight up, and howled, "Hawoooo!!!!!!" I sat in the grass with my mouth wide open in surprise, then began laughing. I'd never heard a dog make such a sound. I howled back. He howled more, and soon we sounded like a pack of two wolves. "You are such a good boy," I said, when our song was finished, my voice gelatinous. "Such a good, good boy."

I'd been with Bunker every minute since I brought him home. The only time I wasn't with him was when I was with my therapist, and I found myself feeling anxious without him, talking about him in her office, thinking of him every few minutes while I was in session. Without him my thoughts took over again, and I wasn't aware enough yet to notice. I wanted to ask my therapist if I could bring Bunker with me, but I couldn't gather the courage.

I liked this therapist, Mya. She was young. She spoke slowly and deliberately, and I found her manner soothing. Her office was a one-story brick building, not far from my parents' house, awash with neutral colors and decorated with crisp photographs of barns and fields from the Ohio countryside.

Mya asked a lot of questions, like "What conclusions did you draw when your friends in New York started to tire of your lovesickness?"

"That I'd be sick of me too," I said.

"But what did that make you think about yourself?"

"I don't know," I said. "That I was a bad friend. That I put all my self-worth into whether this guy still loved me. Just bad, I guess. I felt bad."

"But what were you thinking?"

"That I sucked," I said, tiring of her rapid-fire inquiry.

She put her finger on her nose. I was lost, but she pressed on in this vein. I began to understand that without my realizing it, I perpetually put myself down in my own mind. She called them automatic negative thoughts, and when she said those three words, it was as if a little bell rang in my head. I *did* do that. I always had. But I had never noticed, never thought to question the truth of the negative conclusions I was constantly making. My thoughts ran unhinged for years until I was barely conscious on the kitchen floor, face down on the couch, suicidal. My thoughts blamed me for every problem, put me down whenever possible, and regularly left me shaken, broken, insecure, and mean.

As Mya explained to me, "Your brother long ago stopped being part of your life. He left, went to college, graduated, started his own life that had little to do with yours anymore, right?"

"Right," I said.

"But you have carried on the insults and mistreatment. You now just mistreat yourself." I looked at her with my brow furrowed. This sounded absurd.

I'd visited Clay once, by myself, when he was a senior in college. I was eighteen. It was an awkward but mildly friendly weekend of partying and hanging out. This, we thought, was what brothers and sisters were supposed to do at this age. We weren't exactly close, but he wasn't hideously mean anymore. The plane I took from Ohio to Minnesota was struck by lightning, and when a white burst of light and a deafening bang erupted in the plane's aisle, everyone started screaming. But my thought was *Oh well. I'm ready to die anyway.* I comforted the hysterical eighty-year-old woman next to me but felt startlingly calm. I was eighteen and nonplussed at the idea of dying in a fiery plane crash.

"So," my therapist continued. "You go to New York. Fresh start, right? Except what happens?"

"My boyfriend cheats on me," I said.

"Then what?" she asked.

"Then everything goes to shit," I said.

"Why do you think that happened?" she said.

"Because he defined me," I said.

"And without him?"

"I'm nothing." I looked at the ground. When I said it out loud, it sounded ridiculous. I wore a button on my backpack that said, *This Is What a Feminist Looks Like.* And yet, I felt as if I disappeared if a man didn't love me. What a fraud I was. What a fake, I thought.

"So you ask yourself," Mya said slowly, "is that true? Are you nothing? Are you worthless?"

"No," I said quietly, thinking, *Pretty much, yes.* I had talked to Will the day before, and he told me again how much he loved me, how beautiful I was, how much he missed me. He said he wished things could have ended differently. I told him I agreed.

"No," she echoed. "You are not."

Our time was up, and I walked out of her office with one assignment: Catch a few of my negative thoughts and write them down for our discussion upon my next session.

By the time I got to the car, I had enough material for a few hours' worth of conversation: *Why were you so awkward when you said good-bye? You didn't close the door all the way. Mya wants the door closed, which is why she shut it completely after you left. You made her get up. Your thighs are rubbing together. You're getting fat. You're disgusting. Open the door for that lady, geez. Don't make her wait. Jesus Christ, did you seriously just step on her foot? Apologize to her now.* "Oops! Sorry." *Only you would do something so idiotic. I hope you don't get into a car accident and die on the way home. Because you could, you know. Pay attention to the road. You are a terrible driver. Look before you back out! You learned that years ago! Jesus! You almost hit that guy. Moron.*

On that drive home, from underneath the negative thoughts, bubbled this: *No wonder.* No wonder I've been so down. No wonder I've had a hard time making friends. No wonder New York just about killed me.

The bad thoughts came and went so fast that I didn't notice most of them. But the relief I felt at seeing one nasty thought, and catching it mid-flight was a breakthrough. For the first time since I'd collapsed in that apartment I thought I might be able to get better.

Dog Medicine

Mid-July 1996

Bunker had been with me for three days and we'd established a routine. Wake up, pee, poop, eat, walk, play, nap, and repeat. He was already mostly house-trained. He'd had only one accident on the carpet. I taught him to sit and make eye contact and he did so eagerly, wanting to please, ready for the next command.

Waking up in the morning was getting easier. But something dark still lingered. And on this particular day, for no discernable reason, the darkness reared its ugly head, unannounced, worse than ever, like a thread-thin worm that had covertly dug itself back into my body from underneath a fingernail. It said, *Oh no, you don't. I see you trying to pretend you're happy, trying to fool people that you're not a lazy, ugly idiot.* I felt punished, as if my captor had caught me trying to escape. Perhaps those awful thoughts had never left but just lay dormant for a while. I wanted to fight; I tried hard to push the negativity away, but it persisted.

Just getting a dog can't cure me, I thought. I was the problem. I wasn't strong enough. I was a failure, a crazy person. I was truly unlikeable. I believed this like I believed that the earth was round, something I couldn't see, but understood to be true because I had been told it was so.

I walked to the maroon living room couch and sat down, feeling both afraid and comforted by the re-appearing blackness. Comforted because I knew depression so well. Depression was my companion. The seductive descent into the awful depths marked the return of an old, dark friend that I genuinely, honestly missed.

I had my face in my hands. My body sat small and inert. Breathing became tight, uneven. My parents' great efforts to help me had failed. I had failed. I was so broken. I would never leave home, never keep a job, never be happy. There was no stopping the cascade of terrible, dark, frightening thoughts. Such is the nature of depression; even the most herculean effort to find light and positivity will be extinguished. There seems to be no such thing as solace.

My face was still in my hands when I felt warmth on my toes. Bunker had walked over to me and sat down on my feet. I pulled my hands away from my face and saw him sitting, looking up at me, his butt squarely on my toes, his back leaning into my shins. His face held curiosity, his fevered puppy energy completely contained. He glanced away for a few moments, then turned back, as if to ask, "Better?"

Really? I thought. *Really?* Could this dog somehow sense when I was sad and comfort me? I had heard of seeing-eye dogs. I'd heard of dogs who could sniff out drugs in suitcases. But a dog who could detect sadness? A dog who could sense a down-tick in mood? I wondered if these new psychiatric drugs were causing me to overly anthropomorphize my dog. But I needed so desperately to be comforted. I needed a companion who had no judgment, with whom I had no history, who would make it known that I was loved, who would never, ever hurt me.

So I decided in that moment to trust what I was feeling. Then I remembered the approach that my therapist suggested I try the next time I felt down. She told me not to fight the sorrow. "It's okay to be sad sometimes," she said. "Everyone is sad sometimes. Let the sad feelings in. Be with them. Then see what happens. It's not so bad, right? Ask those dark thoughts: Are you true? Are you real?"

So I decided to be as sad with Bunker as I needed to be, because he didn't care. He accepted me. He didn't need me to be happy. He had witnessed my change in mood, and that alone improved it. He didn't judge me; he simply saw me. So I told myself: *Bunker understands.* But this was a whole new kind of understanding. It was wordless, and it let me be sad until an amazing thing happened: the sadness began to dissolve. I was safe with this dog, and the near instant effect was that the desperation and darkness disappeared, burst in the air like soap bubbles. So I let more sadness in. I felt it. I *really* felt it. Then I petted Bunker and the sorrows didn't seem nearly as big or awful. They even felt untrue. Like, Oh! You're not *really* stupid and ugly and lazy. Of course! You're not *really* hopeless. Are you? No. You are not.

I don't know why it worked. All I can ponder is that this kind of healing required the safety of a true companion, and no resistance. This kind of healing did not want me to fight my sadness. It wanted me to accept it. Welcome it, even. So that the depression could be on its merry fucking way. And Bunker wanted no wrangling of labels to explain my emotional state, my bottomless malaise. He brought only judgment-free listening and wordless faith. When it came to Bunker, I was overflowing with faith. There was something sacred in this dog, connected to the wisdom of nature, but living inside my home. As a child I'd accessed that wordless, wise place so many times during my treks through the woods, and with my beloved dogs Midnight, Blarney, and Cinder. Those places, those dogs had no opinion about themselves, or me, aside from acceptance.

Bunker was still sitting on my feet, still looking at me. His feather-soft fur tickled my legs, and I picked him up, his puppy legs dangling. I cradled his body. He let his tongue drop out the side of his opened mouth. That sight alone made me smile. I leaned back into the couch and held him to my chest. He curled into me as if he felt as protected as I did.

I took a deep breath and felt the blackness loosen its grip. Dog medicine. I'd found it, and I swallowed it whole.

First Lesson

Mid-July 1996

Bunker had a lot to learn. He was mellow for a puppy, but he tugged on the leash, chewed everything in sight, and didn't exactly come when called.

The dog-training book said that dogs who know they're not in charge are relaxed and happy. Their work is only to follow and obey. A dog that is led to believe he's the alpha dog will act out and can become anxious and even aggressive because he is under the illusion that taking care of the pack is his responsibility. I wanted Bunker to know that I was the boss. I would teach him and keep him safe. So I took him outside for some training that would help him see me as his pack leader.

Out in the yard, with a fifteen-foot leash, I followed the book's instructions to walk quietly in a square as big as the yard would allow. I was to hold the leash with two hands at my chest, pay no attention to Bunker, stop at the corners, and just walk in one big, cornered loop. I would use no voice commands and never yank on the leash, just keep walking. If he fell, I would slow down so he could right himself, but otherwise, I was to just walk. The idea was that he would learn, slowly, to stay by my side. I was the alpha. I felt enormously capable of being in charge and taking care of this precious dog.

When I began walking, Bunker was like a housefly on the end of a fishing line, darting in every direction. Instructions for the lesson included avoiding eye contact, but watching peripherally. He spotted a squirrel and raced into the woods after it, then hit the end of the leash, his back feet flipping under his soft puppy body. A bird hopped through beds of leaves at the edge of the woods and Bunker lunged toward it, tripped, and got dragged a few feet. I slowed to let him catch up but didn't acknowledge him. I paused, could feel that he'd righted himself and had begun to walk again, so I sped up. Sometimes he disappeared from my line of sight completely and I had to trust that he was walking and okay, until I felt a pull on the leash.

My mom thought the sight of me dragging my puppy around the yard was funny, so she grabbed the video camera and hid behind a bush, laughing and filming. Bunker caught her scent, and he pulled toward her as I walked in the opposite direction. This resulted in another wipeout and a three-foot dragging through the grass. If my mom thought I'd finally, truly lost my mind, she knew not to say so. She just laughed as I walked, stopped, turned, walked, stopped, turned, and this poor little puppy tried to keep up. I laughed too, at first. But after several rotations, the slow walk became like a meditation. With each turn, I began to realize that Bunker and I were becoming a pack of two. He was learning to trust and follow me, and I was learning that I could lead confidently. When I felt him dragging at the end of the lead, I was terrified I might hurt him, but I began to understand the lesson we were learning: if we were attentive to each other, we would both be okay.

Within about ten minutes, Bunker understood. He trotted at my side, looking up at me to see which way my eyes were turned. He'd figured out that I looked in the direction I was going to go next. His puppy paws lumbered to keep up with me, but he stayed by my side. He wasn't tugging at all now, not getting distracted. I could feel that he was happy to follow me, relieved even. His tail twirled straight up and he walked as if he were proud of himself. When we were done, I stopped, took off the leash, and praised him with a little dancing party in the grass. He ran in circles, barking as I twirled.

When we came inside, he collapsed on the floor with fatigue. I carried him to my room and put him in his crate. I lay on the bed next to him and felt myself drifting off as well. As he fell asleep, he opened his eyes at the slightest noise to make sure I was still close by. "Don't worry, buddy," I said. "I'm right here. I'll always be right here." At that, we both fell into a deep sleep.

Those were such important days. The first few weeks with Bunker set the foundation for our life together. The two of us were braiding our energies. We were tying all of our untied strings together. We lay with each other on warm summer afternoons, slumbering side by side, slowly building a promise to travel this life together. I had no reservations about committing to this dog, because his loyalty, I knew, would never waver. His love for me would not wane. He would remind me, with wagging optimism, of his unbridled love for life, how to be in the present moment and let my troubled thoughts melt away. My only job was to protect and care for him, and I felt confident, despite my shaky mental state, that I could keep him safe, healthy, and loved.

We spent afternoons lying on my bedroom carpet, his shedding puppy hair entwined with my damaged blonde mess. I touched the wet softness of his nose. He licked my finger, then rolled onto his back. When his eyes drooped, I watched his eyelashes flutter long after they closed. I thought of the suicidal plans that used to linger at the edge of my mind. As if a miracle had come, the endless sorrow lost its power with this dog by my side. Something about him began to close that awful chapter of my life.

The days began to pass by steadily. I would wake in the morning feeling the slightest bit of optimism. On sunny days, Bunker and I would go outside and wander through the woods behind the house, his nose working overtime through piles of decomposing leaves, me just ambling, breathing deeply. The leaves were like little healers—all that photosynthesis sending strength through branches that emerged from the trunks that braved the underground, roots spreading out so far through the dirt, farther than we could ever imagine.

Once when I sat down at the base of a tree, Bunker watched

me, perked his ears at my stopping. When he felt my contentedness, he gave a wag of his puppy tail and went about his business
of sniffing, digging his nose deep into the dirt until he found an
earthworm. He'd push his cheek into the ground, then his ear, then
his neck. Finally he'd flop his whole body down onto the ground,
his four legs wiggling wildly skyward, his mouth open and tongue
hanging out as he rubbed the slime of that worm onto his skin.

I never understood why Bunker loved worms so much. But,
I considered, worms invisibly feed the soil. They're good for gar-
dens and make important nutrients for plants to grow. Bunker was
doing this for me. He was feeding me, giving me essential emotional and spiritual nutrients, so I could continue on in my life.
I never once stopped Bunker from rolling in earthworms. It gave
him such pleasure.

CAN'T STAY

AUGUST 2, 1996

I kept my bottle of Zoloft next to the bed and took one pill each morning as soon as I woke up. The medication made me terribly sleepy, and I found myself desperately needing a nap each day at about 11 a.m. Mya suggested I begin taking the pill before bed, so I switched to nighttime, staring at those little yellow oblong pills, wondering what they did for me. I devoured research about how repeated traumas in a young person will induce chronic activation of the hypothalamic-pituitary-adrenal (HPA) axis—the system that directs how a body responds to stress, the "fight or flight" reaction. Tests done in animals showed that if the HPA axis is activated again and again when the brain is still developing, it will forget how to shut off. So the animal lives in constant hyper-vigilance. Even when there is no threat to it, the animal is on high alert— leaving it unable to attend to itself—depleting its energy, its desire for play, food, sex, and interaction. Some researchers say that once this system is activated in humans, it is forever altered, sometimes setting the stage for depression or anxiety that can stay dormant for years, until it finally reveals itself.

The research helped the pieces fall into place. There were reasons that all of this had happened, and it wasn't just that I was a freak or lacked the basic skills to get along in the world. Uncovering those reasons felt like pulling the veil off of a great and mysterious force.

The fact was, I was recovering. I could feel it. Therapy was slowly helping, the medication seemed to be working, and I had

Bunker. I made a daily practice of noticing my thoughts as I walked my dog. Those two acts helped me notice, feel, then dissolve the depressive, heavy, black thoughts.

Still, ever persistent in the back of my mind was the nagging unknown of what I would do next, where I would go. My dad would always say, "There's no pressure here, but we would just *love* it if you stayed close to home." The truth was that living in Ohio had always felt wrong, like I didn't belong. I remember driving on the outer-belt that encircles Columbus, looking into other cars and wondering if there was someone out there like me in this town. I'm sure there was, but I hadn't found them.

Despite this, I wanted to at least consider making a life for myself in Ohio. So one afternoon, my mom and I put Bunker in the car and drove to a local dog-friendly apartment complex we'd found in the newspaper. The unit sat in a squat one-story brick apartment building near the Scioto River. We walked into the damp living room with a sour-smelling brown carpet, thin walls, and chipping Formica kitchen counters, and turned right around. We didn't need to say much to each other in the car, other than "Nope. Not going to work." My fears reared up. Was this what life was like for me now? Moldy, drafty, lonely apartments with paper-thin walls? An office job I would loathe that kept me inside all day pushing papers and tapping on a computer under fluorescent lights? My parents had paid my first month's rent in New York. After that, it was up to me. That year I lived in New York City, I didn't have enough money for a warm coat. It also happened to be during the Northeast's blizzard of 1996, and it wasn't until I broke down crying inside an Eddie Bauer store at Christmas time that my mother gave in and bought me a thick down parka, passing me a handwritten I.O.U. and due date on the back of the receipt. My parents wanted self-sufficiency. I wanted that too, and the thought of it simultaneously enlivened me and made me fear that I would end up in a place far worse than the moldy, drafty apartment by the river.

Bunker stayed close to me after we returned home. I had

already begun to count on him sensing my mood. A stroke down his back brought me a deep breath. Sitting down next to him on the floor leveled my nerves, brought me back to zero, out of the negative thoughts. Watching him race around the room in a wild puppy frenzy negated my worry.

Bunker's presence felt as necessary as oxygen to me, and I began to panic at the thought of working again, leaving him for eight or more hours every day. Then a deep sigh from him would pull a long intake of breath from me, followed by a slow exhale that calmed my jangled nerves. Instead of whirling myself into a fit of anxiety and terror followed by surrender and then depression, I would just stop. Take a deep breath. Slow down. Pet Bunker. Don't think. Just be. It could be okay. Just maybe it would all turn out okay.

That afternoon the phone rang. My mom answered and said, "Sure, she's right here." I hadn't received a phone call from a friend in months, and couldn't imagine who it was. The only person who had intermittently called me was Will, and those calls were usually after midnight. I pointed, silently, questioning, at my chest.

"Hello?" I said, tentative. Was it my therapist? My old boss? Leah?

"Hey, it's Melissa!" It took me a while to place who Melissa was. I listened and remembered her voice. She was a friend from high school that I'd known since preschool but with whom I wasn't all that close. She'd gone to college in Maine and we'd kept in touch with occasional phone calls and letters, but nothing significant. She was one of those friends who was good at staying connected, though, so I wasn't terribly surprised to hear from her.

"My mom told me you were living in Ohio again," she said. "How'd *that* happen?" She said this like my landing home was an unfortunate turn of events, and I took it as an insult and wanted to hang up. Instead, I walked to my bedroom with the cordless phone and said, "Well," I paused. "I pretty much hated New York."

"Oh," she said. "Doesn't everyone? When I was at Bowdoin, everyone got jobs so that they *wouldn't* have to live in New York.

Not at this stage in life, anyway." I sat down feeling immense, toppling relief. Because a depressed person will build up such an invisible wall in preparation for feeling hurt that when someone shows that such a wall isn't necessary, the reprieve from the hard work of self-defense is enormous.

"Yeah," I said, mumbling. "Guess I didn't get that memo."

"Well," she continued, "I somehow ended up way out in Seattle. I did an internship with a clothing company here when I was in college and I'm back out here doing marketing for them. Seattle's a pretty cool town. I like it so far," she said.

"That's cool," I said. "My aunt lives there. I love visiting her." I sat on my bed and fiddled with the lacey edge of my white comforter. This kind of small talk made me antsy. How meaningless it felt compared to all I was going through. Still, I continued. "I was working at a publisher in New York. It was cool, I guess." I paused. "Well, not really."

"No, sounds *totally* cool," she said. "I'm living by myself right now, which is fine, but I'm moving soon."

"Cool," I said, flustered because I had nothing else to add.

"Where are you going next?" she asked. "Are you staying in Columbus?" Her tone held a lack of judgment, an open-mindedness.

"I have no idea," I said, holding my breath, then laughing a little bit too loud. Bunker looked up at me. Calm.

"Seattle's pretty nice," she said, her voice lilting, like she was offering me a tempting treat.

"Do you have other friends out there?" I asked.

"Yeah, a few. And I have a boyfriend now. But it would be totally awesome to have more friends like you close by." She was being so *nice*. Had her mother somehow found out that I'd had a breakdown and told her to call me and check in? Why would she want me to come live in Seattle?

"Yeah," I mumbled.

"Seriously," she said. "I'm moving into a house with a friend of mine, this guy named Chris. And I think his friend Greg is going to move in with us too. We're house hunting right now. Then when we find a house, we totally want to get a dog. Seattle is super dog-friendly."

"Really?" I said, wondering if perhaps this was a practical joke.

"Oh, yeah," she said. "Dogs everywhere. And we all totally miss having one."

"Well, you won't believe this. I just got a puppy," I said. Bunker was snoozing on my bedroom floor and opened his eyes a sliver when I said his name.

"No way!" she said, laughing in a way that seemed out of proportion to the conversation. Or maybe it wasn't. I couldn't tell anymore. "Then you definitely need to move out here! It'd be a perfect fit!"

"Really?" I said. "That could be an option."

"Seriously? You'd consider it?" she said.

I assumed she'd gotten in over her head, really didn't mean to ask me to live with her in Seattle. "I don't want to invite myself," I said.

"What? No! It'd be so amazing if you actually moved out here. I mean, seriously, it would be epic! We would have so much fun." Clearly she didn't know who I'd become in this last year. I made a mental note to make sure she never talked to my New York friends, who would describe me as anything but fun.

"Okay," I said. I rubbed my forehead with my palm, squeezed my eyes shut. Exhaustion threatened.

"How about this," she said. "You take a day or two. Think about it. We haven't started house hunting yet. When we do, we'll either look for a three- or four-bedroom place, depending on what you decide. Simple as that!" She laughed again. "Man, that would be so awesome!"

I couldn't figure this out. Was she actually lonely and miserable out there in the rain? Did she need someone to come so far west to quell her isolation? We were friends in high school but not great friends. Melissa was much more popular than me; she had another best friend with whom she spent nearly every waking minute. They had the kind of best friendship I'd always envied. Why was she interested in hanging out with me now?

There was an awkward pause before I finally replied, "Let me talk to my parents. See what they think. I guess I have nothing to lose at this point." The words seemed to come from behind me. I almost turned around to check the flowered wallpaper for someone whispering words into my ear. What was I saying?

I feared that I was failing to match Melissa's enthusiasm (a sentiment I hadn't felt in months), so I rather abruptly ended the phone call. After I hung up, I imagined that Melissa was like a customer at a used-car lot. I was a familiar brand of car, but she had no idea I was such a lemon. The next second, I dismissed the idea of moving entirely.

I went back to the kitchen. My mom stood at the stove. The afternoon light pooled on the kitchen counter, the leaves outside the window glistened. "Who was that?" she asked, dropping white onions into an oiled pan.

"Melissa," I said. "I wonder how she knew I was home." My mom shrugged, then asked how Melissa was doing. I considered not telling her that I'd just been invited to move to Seattle. I could just forget about it. Keep it to myself so that I didn't have to make a decision. Bunker trotted into the kitchen. Melissa said Seattle was dog-friendly. I thought of my mom's youngest sister who lived there, my aunt who loved animals the way I did, and the words tumbled out without further consideration. "She invited me to move to Seattle and live with her and two guys." My mom froze, then looked up from the vegetables she was chopping. "And they were thinking about getting a dog. So if I come, they won't need to. They'd love Bunker."

She set her knife down. "Oh, honey, I know they would," she said. "Wow. Seattle."

We looked at each other, considering this new direction for my life, a genuine opportunity blossoming from a surprise phone call.

"Wow," she said again. We heard a skittering of claws in the living room and Bunker was chasing Cinder again. Cinder was baring her teeth and Bunk was down on his front haunches, inviting her to play. She barked at him, charged him, and he backed into the cabinet, tail between his legs. Cinder trotted over to the red couch, hopped up, and put her chin between her paws, watching this uninvited puppy warily. Bunker's moment of fear had dissipated by the time I reached for him, picked him up, and held him in my arms. "You gotta learn, buddy," I said. "She rules the roost. And she doesn't like playing."

"Cinder's miserable," my mom said, laughing. "She's saying, 'Who on earth is that annoying *thing,* and when is he *leaving?*'" When my mom said this, it felt like the first gentle nudge back out of the nest. Bunker and I weren't going to be living here forever. We could leave, and now we even had a place to go.

"Totally," I responded, taking another look at Cinder still parked on the couch. She was angry, blinking, so unhappy about sharing the attention. "Totally true."

The List of Pros and Cons

August 5, 1996

Three days had passed since Melissa called. I sat in my room late on the night I was supposed to call and tell her whether I wanted to move in with her and her friends. It was midnight in Ohio, 9 p.m. in Seattle. Not too late to call, but I was nowhere near a decision. Bunker lay curled in his crate with the door open. I'd been reinforcing his recall all day, and he was exhausted with a belly full of treats.

My bedroom window was cracked open, and in spilled my favorite sounds, the crickets and cicada and owl calls, the symphony of a summer night in Ohio. They were a loud chorus, messy but still somehow in unison, a warm lullaby that I'd taken for granted as a child. In New York, I remember perking up when I heard one lonely cricket in the bush outside my apartment. I wondered how he ended up stranded in that endless metropolis. I mourned for him that no female would ever answer the call of his rubbing legs, and I wrote a really bad poem about his plight.

I sat in front of Bunker's open crate, thinking about this new possibility. I closed my eyes, took a deep breath, asked the crickets to give me an answer. Should I go? Were there crickets at night in Seattle? Was this all too soon? Was I ready to try again?

I heard the shuffle of my mom's slippers in the kitchen, the clinking of dishes, the rumble of the starting dishwasher. She and my dad had been watching television, and my dad had just gone to bed. He didn't say it, but I knew he thought Seattle was too far away, too risky for my fragile emotional state. It was dark and rainy, he said, and I had no job there. "But whatever you want to do, I will support," he said, though his voice was unconvincing, and I knew he wanted me to stay.

"Hey, there." My mom peeked her head into my bedroom.

"Hi," I greeted her, then turned back to the open window.

"Beautiful night," she said, pulling her robe tight around her waist.

I had been daydreaming about Will in New York, imagining what he was doing, who he was kissing.

My mom sat down next to me on the floor. She smelled like dish-soap and perfume. In her presence, for whatever reason, I had a momentary panic that I was on the precipice of feeling depressed again. Could I possibly move to *another* new town? Could I try again? I thought of Melissa's enthusiasm on the phone.

"I don't know what to do," I said. "I was supposed to call Melissa today and now it's probably too late."

"I'm sure she can wait until tomorrow," my mom said. She seemed so sure, but I was stuck. "Do you want to make a list?" she asked. Forever the taskmaster, my mother walked to my desk, grabbed a red pen and a yellow pad of paper. She patted my sheets, summoning me to my bed. "Okay," she said, drawing a line down the middle of the page. The clock read 12:08.

"Aren't you tired?" I asked.

"Nah," she said. "Let's get thinking here. Pros of going to Seattle and cons of going to Seattle. Go."

I spoke, she wrote. By the end of our brainstorming session, we had an impressive list with barely a few more pros than cons. My mom promised she would drive out west with me, had written "Mom/Daughter Thelma and Louise road trip" on the "pros" side. The list seemed make-believe. I just kept wondering if I was well enough to even attempt to make it out in the world again. My mom handed me the list, her just-now-aging hands pointing to each item. "Can live with Aunt Aurora initially," was listed as a pro.

"Did Aunt Aurora say I could live with her for a few weeks?" I asked.

"I haven't asked her yet, but I know she'd love to have you," my mom said. Aurora, my mom's youngest sister, was the one family member I felt understood me. She was a therapist who seemed to actually see the problems within my family when everyone else either ignored them or thought we were perfectly fine. Aurora had a dog, a few cats, and a rabbit, and she rode horses with her daughters almost every day. She would adore Bunker, I knew it.

"I don't know," I said. "What should I do?" A glance at the clock showed 1:30 a.m.

"I say you go for it," she said. We both smiled, and I felt a surge of happiness followed closely by panic.

"I should move?" I said.

"Look," she held my hands in hers. "I would love for you to stay close to us forever, but Ohio isn't the right place for you." Her chin quivered. "I wish it was, but it isn't. So you have to explore. You have to get out there. I say go for it."

My mom, who I'd only seen cry once, wiped away a tear as she squeezed my hands. "I'll feel much better about this because Aunt Aurora is there," she said, sniffing. "You have family there who you can go to if you need anything. And, you know, Aurora's a therapist so she totally gets it." A month ago, were my mom to suggest that I needed regular therapeutic intervention, I would've been insulted. But now I knew she simply cared, and I also knew that needing help wasn't a bad thing. My mom and dad insisted that my depression wasn't a character flaw or something to fear. "It's just your brain's chemistry," my dad would say, over and over again, until the need for Zoloft seemed as normal as the need for daily vitamins. I was slowly realizing that their acceptance of my illness was a gift.

"Okay," I said, as if amazed by the word. "Okay. I'll go. I'll move to Seattle. I'll try again." My mom smiled, put her hands over her mouth, and gave a little yelp. Bunker startled awake. "Want to go for a car ride, Bunk?" I asked.

Part II

Howl

August 1996

The miles rolled beneath us. I watched the flat horizon and kept one hand on Bunker's crate. We had managed to squeeze the crate into the backseat of my used Ford Explorer, reasoning that since the metal doghouse was his safe place inside our house, he might feel less displaced if he spent much of our weeklong drive tucked inside.

Through much of western Ohio, I sat twisted in the passenger seat, looking backward at my boy. It was as if I couldn't look forward yet. I couldn't look ahead at what might happen in Seattle. What if surviving on my own there was as difficult as it was in New York? I tried to push away the fear that I'd end up depressed again, that I would make all the same mistakes. I hadn't called Will to tell him I was moving. His calls, his professions of love were becoming routine, but I didn't know how to refuse him. Part of me loved hearing him say that he loved me, that my body was his favorite, that he missed it like crazy.

In the car, I watched this little animal behind the bars of his crate. His limbs were getting longer, but his face was still puppyish. He looked at me with wide-eyed concern for the first several hours of the drive, as if to say: Do you know that the room is *moving*?

Soon he resigned himself to this strange place and lay down, resting his chin on his paws and drifting in and out of sleep. Somewhere around Indiana, to keep him engaged as my mom drove, I started to howl and bark at him. Every once in a while, he would bark too and I'd push a treat between the bars of the crate.

My mom chuckled as I repeatedly said, "Speak!" in a high-pitched voice. She must have known that Bunker and I were deepening our language, cementing our understanding of one another. After a while, he began to howl happily after a few barks. "Hawooo-oo-oo!" he would cry, then wag his tail and look at me, as if he were proud and expecting a treat and my reply. I'd howl back and he'd join me. Before long, all three of us were a chorus of voices, like wolf ancestors meeting in a beige SUV. My mom's howl came out high and polite, like she was singing in a church pew. But she was howling with us, and that thrilled me. "Amazing," my mom said. "Have you ever heard a dog howl like that?"

"It's so expressive," I said. "Like if you played it backwards on a record player, you'd hear a complete sentence."

"Totally," she said. "It's uncanny."

We watched the road for a bit, and then every once in a while, I would howl. Within a moment, Bunker would grumble back or howl in return. Communication had commenced. Bunker had long howls, happy howls, and howls crackling with longing. I imagined I could understand them all. When it came to Bunker, I had chosen to trust myself.

My mom and I were good road-trip partners. She tolerated my musical choices (all Ani DiFranco, all the time), and I obliged her occasional request for silence. We drove with the windows down much of the time. The changes in smell signaled our movement: In Indiana, flowers and sulfur and exhaust. Illinois, the slight scent of wheat, ground corn ebbing from the coming plains. Missouri, scorched asphalt mixed with cut grass and cow dung.

As was our way, we didn't talk of anything substantive. No deep discussions, no emotion, no gut spilling. My mother was taking care of me, giving to me, in the way she knew best—with all her time and attention. The absence of intense conversation was welcome at this point in my recovery. I had been wrung dry by the breakdown, by the summer of falling deeper and deeper, and by the proverbial hands of therapists, parents, and doctors who had sought to pull me back up. I was ready for some emotional radio silence.

Across the quiet plains of Nebraska at dusk, I put the pillow against the window and thought about language and speaking and silence. Bunker would learn to speak alongside me. I would learn to speak up for what I wanted, to trust what I felt, to give it weight and importance, to ask for help. I would take care of Bunker, and Bunker would be my constant and loyal companion. My devotion to him was a salve, the only thing I knew for sure.

I made grand, optimistic plans with each westerly beat and fought away the still omnipresent but not nearly as believable negative voices in my mind. I imagined us as pioneers moving westward, the three of us chasing the sun every night like we might actually be able to catch it.

FALLING IN SUN VALLEY
AUGUST 1996

My mom's middle sister, Diane, owned a house in Sun Valley, Idaho, so we planned a detour there. We would enjoy a day of rest before the final push toward Seattle. Aunt Diane was in California while we were there, so we had the house to ourselves. We arrived in the dark and fumbled with the key under the dim porch light where the bodies of moths pinged against the bulb. Bunker perked his ears. I imagined him sensitive even to the pain of insects.

The door creaked open and the house breathed musty on us, a long exhale of dust after months of being uninhabited. We had spent a Christmas at this house when I was a teenager. I had fine memories of a horse-drawn sleigh ride, ice-skating, games of Tile Rummy with my cousins, aunts, uncles, and grandparents. I had all girl cousins, two of them from California who were beautiful, blonde, and my age. They had a deep sisterly bond. I couldn't fathom having a sister. I couldn't fathom not feeling adrift in relation to my sibling. I longed for what they had, not even sure that I understood exactly what it was.

But mostly, my conclusion after that Christmas was that they were cool, smart rebels—and I was not. They were quiet, rolled their eyes regularly, dug Aerosmith, and wore black rubber jewelry. I was too visibly excited to unwrap the new Dee-Lite CD signed "From Santa." Their hair was long, blonde, and stringy straight. They wore two-day-old black eyeliner while I still had a perm and was prone to wearing my hair up in a denim scrunchie at the top of my head. They wore paper-thin, ripped white men's T-shirts even though it was snowing outside. I wore my royal blue turtleneck under a purple, red, and blue machine-made sweater.

I sat on the living room couch and shivered away those memories of that Christmas. Bunker climbed next to me and put his head on my lap. Re-envisioning childhood discomforts felt akin to walking through a beautiful wildflower field full of land mines. You never knew when a nice evening walk could become an unprecedented disaster.

My mom was rushing by me, wanting to unload the car and get to bed. I watched her. She hunched over when she was hurrying, like she was cold or suffered from osteoporosis or really needed to pee. I longed to talk to her about that Christmas, about how it shook my confidence, about how I let tiny little events like small glances from my cousins steal away bits of my self-worth, and there wasn't much there to begin with. My therapist in Ohio had told me that it made sense that I was struggling. "Anyone who has been through what you've been through would be struggling," she said.

But what was it that I had been through, really? I still came back to that question. I still couldn't quite piece together what had rendered me unable to function. What left me so broken? Was I simply a weak person? A lot of people fought with their siblings. Were society's messages to girls—that we need to be good and beautiful and kind and quiet—to blame? Were my parents to blame? Was Clay? I didn't say good-bye to him when I left Ohio. He was happy in his engagement, looking to buy his first house and begin his life as an adult. Was there no one to blame after all? Was blame not at all the point here?

"Coming to bed?" my mom asked, half up the stairs.

"What?" I said.

"Come on," she said, a little impatient. "It's late. Let's sleep."

"Okay," I said, patting Bunker, who still rested his head on my lap. "Come on, boy," I said, whispering, "I'm okay." And with that, he hopped up, climbed the stairs, and settled on a shag rug next to my bedside for a quiet night's sleep under the bright and clear Idaho moon.

The next day we decided to go for a hike. It was a beautiful summer morning, warm but not hot and almost no humidity. We drove up a dirt road and the car dusted to a stop at the trailhead that Aunt Diane promised would lead to a stunning hike up a verdant, wildflowered hill.

We trudged up the trail, rocks crunching underfoot, butterflies and bees twirling around flower heads. "Can you believe we've already driven two thousand miles?" my mom said, hiking behind me. Bunker walked in front of us looking back regularly to ensure we were coming. "Six hundred miles or so to go. More than two-thirds of the way there!"

"I know," I said. "Crazy." I liked our gradual change in longitude. The slow, perpetual movement felt good. I unlatched Bunker's red leash and draped it over my shoulder then clasped it across my chest. I swiveled my baseball hat backwards and walked up the gentle hill flanked by enormous oaks like giant umbrellas, thigh-tall grasses, and flowers swaying in the breeze. Bunker ran as fast as his puppy legs would take him. He led the way up the trail, always stopping to look back. Just watching him run free made bursts of happiness flash through me. I found myself laughing, closing my eyes, turning my face up to the sun, thinking, *Thank you.*

We walked a few miles, then turned around and descended, hungry for lunch. Bunker was limping a little, but I assumed he was simply worn out. I checked his paws for thorns: nothing. My mom snapped a picture of Bunker and me after we'd begun the descent back to the car. Later, after the picture was developed, I could see that he didn't look okay. At the time, we chalked up his funny gait to exhaustion from a healthy run in the mountains. After all, this was a dog from the flatlands of Ohio. He'd never trudged up a mountain before. That night, he slept on the cool brick of the fireplace's hearth, flattened on his side, completely spent.

Then the next morning, after we woke and stuffed the car for our last long leg of the trip, Bunker couldn't stand up. "Come on, Bunk," I called as my mom rinsed our breakfast dishes. "Potty!" He tried to get up but couldn't. The little furry dots above his eyes read: *Confused. Pain.*

My mom walked out of the kitchen. "What's wrong?" she said, wiping her hands on a dish towel.

"I don't know," I said. "He just whimpers when he tries to get up. He's hurt somewhere." I gently squeezed his back left leg and he squealed wildly, searingly, in pain. "Oh shit," I whispered. Adrenaline made my ears ring.

My mom had her hand over her mouth, then began panicking aloud. "We made him do too much. Oh, my gosh. I wonder if he broke all his paws." I closed my eyes, tried to focus, leaned down, and picked him up. I carried him outside. "I can't believe we did that!" my mom cried. "He's only a puppy! What were we thinking taking him on such a long walk?"

"He's okay," I said, as my insides churned with worry. I carried him to the grass and put him down, my mom pacing behind me. He put no pressure on his feet, simply fell to the ground.

"Oh, my god," she said. "He can't walk. What should we do? Should I call Diane and try to find an emergency vet in Sun Valley?"

"Mom!" I yelled. This was *my* dog. My lifeline. I wanted her freaked-out energy away from us. "Just give us a minute. Finish packing and I'll sit with him." She held her clenched fist to her mouth before sighing and stepping back into the house to finish loading the dishwasher.

I felt Bunker's legs, his paw pads rough and tender under my fingers. He whined, then licked my hand when I lightly squeezed his back right paw. I had no idea what was wrong, but I couldn't bear that I'd inadvertently hurt him. "Oh, buddy," I whispered. "What happened? What did we do?" He tried to get up, stood unsteadily to pee, then fell down again in the grass. I imagined how deeply I would fall if I lost him. This recovery was only going as well as it was because I could turn to Bunker in moments of desperation. Without him, I knew I would be back in the darkness. Without him, I knew I would not likely survive.

When my mom came back outside, Bunker's eyes were closed and I was petting him, the only sound the house's wind chime clinking in the morning breeze. She put her hand on my shoulder and said, "He'll be okay, Julie."

I nodded, pushed my hands under his belly, and loaded him into the car. We drove in silence for about twenty miles before my mom began pontificating about the injury. "He probably just bruised his paw pads," she said, both hands on the steering wheel, eyes straight ahead. I nodded. "He'll be fine," she said. "We'll take him to the vet when we get to Seattle, make sure everything's okay." I put those words on replay in my mind and watched the earth undulate beneath us.

Aunt Aurora's House

August 1996

The final day's drive felt quick. We'd left Sun Valley and drove almost eight hours before spending the night near Moses Lake, Washington. We woke the next morning, excited because it was only three more hours to Seattle. We tumbled across the Columbia River at ten o'clock, the loping hills and coming mountains promising something different. I felt like a homing pigeon following a magnetic field. Something already felt right about Seattle, like it would go easier on me than New York.

We were quiet as we peaked the evergreen-laden mountains, speeding our way through Snoqualmie Pass. The impossible green richness of the hills seemed to fill me with hope, like the greener the world became, the happier I felt. With all that rain in Seattle, I thought, I'm going to be ecstatic.

On the drive, at rest stops, I carried Bunker to pee. He didn't seem unhappy, but he was not his usual energetic, goofy self. Still, his mobility seemed to slowly improve with each stop. It seemed fortuitous that yesterday and most of today, he was required to stay in his crate and rest except for occasional pit stops.

Three hours later we climbed my aunt's narrow two-lane road canopied by enormous pines and flanked by ferns of prehistoric proportions. I noticed that my palms were sweating. When we pulled up to Aurora's house, the front door was wide open. My foot was on the driveway before the car was completely stopped. We'd made it. An orange and white cat curled around the doorframe, then sped under a bush when Brandy the Brittany spaniel careened through the doorway, barreling, tail twirling, toward our car. My fingers jangled nervous energy as I watched the door for my aunt. She didn't appear, so I greeted the animals first, a much less formidable task. I loved my aunt Aurora, but greeting anyone was difficult for me: the sudden rush of emotion, the hugs, the high-pitched hellos. My upper lip would sweat; my ears would ring.

I lifted Bunker out of his crate and as soon as his paws hit the ground, it was clear he was feeling better. He greeted Brandy with his body erect, his tail a circling flag. Then four doggie elbows down on the ground and they were off, playing like old friends. They chased each other in the front yard and Bunker paused hastily to pee, still a puppy that didn't lift his leg.

"I wonder where Aurora is," my mom said. "The door's open. Aurora!" she yelled. The house was a fifties-era ranch built into a gentle hill on a quiet street. On clear days, the porch off the living room boasted views of the Cascade Mountains. It was one of those houses that look like they'd just grown out of the ground—all rock and wood and green plants. Inside, it smelled musty, like animals, a little bit like a barn: hay and feed and animal hair.

"I'm here!" came a voice from inside the darkened doorway. It was a sunny day in Seattle. The clerk at the gas station east of Snoqualmie had joked that we were going to arrive just in time for Seattle's three days of summer. Aurora appeared in the door-way, her hair in an orange bandanna, hands in green garden gloves blackened with dirt. There was a smear of soil on her forehead. She gave us a closed-mouth, head-tilted smile and opened her arms. I hugged her awkwardly. I felt light-headed so sat down on a con-crete bench next to a fountain that was caked with bright-green algae. Brandy trotted up to the fountain and slurped some murky water.

"Is that okay?" I asked, imagining dirt and grime sliding down his gullet.

"Oh, sure," she said. "Good minerals in there." She peeled off her gloves and looked at me. I thought about Aurora as a therapist, transported her to my own therapist's chair. What would she say about what a mess I'd been?

Mom and I settled into the guest room, then ate a quiet dinner with Aurora, my uncle Bob, and their two daughters, one in middle school and one in high school. I loved this family, always had. They felt solid. Aurora seemed to genuinely listen to her kids. I watched as she spoke to them in a language that seemed all their own. I could tell that they talked a lot. My uncle Bob was a soft-spoken former hippie, a thoughtful man. Watching them made me feel like an alien coming to a lovely new planet, one where dad came home at the same time every night, where mom was emotionally involved with her kids, where the kids didn't fight to the death.

It was my mom who first said, "Aurora, you're going to have to be Julie's surrogate mother while she's living here." I beamed at this idea. If my mom felt threatened by her depressed daughter happily living in her sister's house, she never expressed it. She only showed support, and for that I was grateful.

After a few days at Aurora's, it was time for my mom to fly back to Ohio. Bunker and I drove her to the airport and pulled up to the departures curb. I couldn't imagine the passenger seat without my mom, but she seemed ready to go home. She said she missed Cinder and that Dad had probably eaten peanut butter sandwiches for the entire week she was gone. "That and chocolate chips," I said.

"Exactly," she said, laughing and opening the car door. I pulled her suitcase out from the back of the truck and put it on the sidewalk. "Let me say good-bye to Bunk first," she said. She opened the backseat door and hugged him like he was her own son. She whispered something into his ear, held his head with both her hands, and kissed the bridge of his nose.

"I'm gonna miss that dog," she said.

"Mom," I said, taking her hands. "I think I'm going to be okay here. I really do. Thank you for everything you've done for me. I love you. So much."

"You are going to be so happy," she said. "I just know it."

"Thank you, Mama," I said, through the massive lump in my throat. "I love you."

She hugged me and gave me a quick kiss. "Listen," she said, holding both my hands. "Let's do the same thing we did when you were away at college. Let's look at the moon. Remember? When you see the moon, know that I'm looking at the same moon you are, no matter where we are. It's the same moon shining on us. Okay?" she said. We'd done this when I spent a semester abroad in Australia while I was in college, and we'd done it when I went to Italy on a high school exchange program. It was my mom's way of connecting us despite any distance. "I'll call you when I get home. Have *fun*, Julie. You're going to do wonderful things."

With that, she blew me a kiss, turned around, and rushed through the airport's sliding doors. I took a deep breath and walked around my car. I buckled my seat belt as tears came. Big tears. I wiped my eyes, wondering if I was making a huge mistake. I missed my mom terribly already. Then Bunker jumped from the backseat into the passenger seat, opened his mouth and let his long pink tongue dangle carelessly, so I laughed through my tears.

"Okay, buddy," I said. "I get it. No lingering all sad at the departures curb. Let's get on with it. Here we go." I put the car in drive, pressed the gas and rested my right hand on Bunker's back as I drove past the city back to Aunt Aurora's house.

Foster Child

August 1996

Aurora loved Bunker. She sat down on the ground with him and let his puppy paws climb all over her. She got orange dog hair all over her clothes, let him lick her cheek and sniff her ears with intensity. Animals loved her. They spoke to her in a way I knew well. All my life my mom had suggested that Aurora was a little odd for how much she loved animals, her endless parade of guinea pigs and cats and dogs as a kid. Animals were her childhood solace in a world that made her feel alone and not good enough. Just like me. She was the youngest of three, with two over-achieving sisters. She had a wandering eye as a child and struggled through surgeries and glasses while her older sister, my mother, was the homecoming queen, and her middle sister was the blonde athlete of the family. I remember hearing jokes about how she was supposed to be a boy. Part of her always felt she'd failed before she was even born, her father's last failed attempt at a son.

I think Bunker sensed Aurora's deep connection to animals and the natural world. He listened intently to her, loved her with a heart-crackling clarity that I understood was from the depths, from far, far below what we understand to be visible in this world. The three of us seemed to congregate there.

Those nights at Aurora's, we'd sit on the couch flanked by cats and dogs, her rabbit Radar sleeping soundly on her chest. We'd just be together. I got to feel a different kind of mothering. It wasn't better than my mom's—just more my frequency. Like Seattle. A better-fitting longitude. We spent time together with no small talk. Only real talk. Emotions were not a taboo subject in this house. In fact, they were almost always the topic of conversation. Aurora told me, for the first time, that depression and alcoholism ran in my family. I learned that everyone knew my immediate family's problems, despite no one's ever mentioning them to me. I felt a reckoning, a peace. Maybe I wasn't so weak and crazy after all.

Melissa and I connected on the phone and made plans to have dinner with the guys, the other two soon-to-be roommates who also were friends from high school in California. We all went to different colleges and graduated in 1995. One guy was in graduate school and the other was working downtown at a film company.

I talked to the grad-school guy on the phone to plan our first meeting. I told him I'd pick him up outside his building on the University of Washington's campus. He said his name was Greg and that he'd be the guy in the plaid shirt waiting on Fifteenth Avenue. "What color plaid?" I asked.

"Well, let me see." I could hear by his voice that he was looking down at his chest. "Red, yellow, blue, green, a little bit of, I don't know, purple?" he said.

"Any more colors?" I said. "Because that'll make it much more specific."

He laughed. I bit my nails sitting on Aurora's carpeted living room stairs. She stood in the kitchen, cooking pasta for her daughters. The bunny scratched his ear just outside the sliding glass door. Bunker slept at my feet. And I had just made a boy laugh.

Not long after my mom left, the infamous Seattle clouds crept in. Days and days of gray-white skies, cool temperatures, and intermittent drizzle. But the gray came as a surprising comfort to me. Seattle felt like a gentle friend, taking me in her arms, holding me with her dim light, making my re-entry into the world a quiet, slow, easy one. I loved the clouds. They made me feel as if a blanket were wrapped around me. It wasn't always sunny all the time, and that was okay. A place can still be beautiful, breathtaking even, when it's gray and damp. The flourishing plants, the animals thriving there, they all spoke so much more than the sun could. Like the roots of a tree, hidden underground and more elaborate and astounding than we would ever know.

BLIND ROOMMATES

AUGUST 1996

On a Friday afternoon, I kissed Bunker good-bye, left Aunt Aurora's house, and drove to the University of Washington to pick up Greg. The housemates were meeting for the first time, gathering at a pub for beer and burgers. I pulled up to the sidewalk at the university and spotted him. The plaid shirt was indeed just about every color but pink and I chuckled as he circled my car and opened the passenger door.

"Sounds like you need new brakes," he said. "I'm Greg." He was right. The brakes on my truck had been squeaking since Missouri.

"I know," I said. "Good thing I made it cross-country. I'm Julie." We shook hands. I laughed a little; he was cute. Melissa was not exaggerating when she said he had the bluest eyes she'd ever seen. He had dark hair, beautiful full lips, and black lashes that made his eyes stand out like lit-from-behind gemstones. I wanted to keep looking at him, but I forced myself to watch the road. "This is weird," I said, pushing my hair behind my ear and flicking the turn signal. "It's like we're all on a blind roommates date." He laughed and adjusted his backpack between his legs.

"That's because we kind of are," he said, smiling, confident. We chatted for the rest of the drive about what he was studying (molecular biology, whatever that is), and where he grew up (Northern California). I told him about my year in New York and about how I was looking forward to living in a real house with a real yard because I had a dog. A great dog. A dog he would love.

"Can't wait to meet him," he said. "I really wanted to get a dog, but I'm at the lab too much, so this works out perfectly."

Driving down from Aurora's house, I had contemplated my last few months: the depression, the medication and therapy, Bunker's companionship giving me enough courage to try something new. I vacillated between hope and dread; sure one minute that the housemates would love me, sure the next that we'd hate each other and I'd be forced to crawl back to Ohio defeated again. But when I met Greg, there was a simple calm, like a leaf floating to the ground, or maybe rather an enormous 767 landing with a barely perceptible touch. There was a peace about him, a surefootedness that I found comforting. I knew we would be friends.

We parked and met Melissa outside the pub. I hadn't seen her in a few years and she looked fantastic; slim with her normally bobbed hair lopped into a pixie cut. She introduced me to our other roommate, Chris, a tall Nordic-looking guy who hugged me tight upon our meeting. The four of us slid into a booth made of dark wood, sour with the smell of old beer. Everyone seemed a little nervous and I wondered how Bunker was doing without me. My mind wandered to various scenarios: my cousins accidentally letting him out the front door, him getting hit by a car, a horrific scene looping through my mind's eye. I tried to fight the thoughts away and listen to my new housemates. Melissa ordered four glasses and a pitcher, then poured us each a golden-brown beer. She held up her glass. "Here's to our new place," Melissa said. "It's going to be awesome."

We drank and talked about our first years out of college. Melissa had lived in an apartment by herself. Greg too. Greg had gone to Princeton and was in his first year of grad school. Chris had gone to Davidson, graduated, and spent a year traveling in Africa. He gestured wildly with his hands when he spoke and laughed from deep in his belly. I told them I had spent the year in Manhattan but realized East Coast big-city life wasn't for me. Greg said he'd decided that living alone wasn't for him, that he was excited to have roommates. Chris said living in Kenya had changed his life forever.

They asked about my road trip, and as I spoke, I felt that we were like four pegs in a board, all sliding into place. Gathered around that dented, sticky table, I don't think I was the only one who felt a surge of hope, as if somehow the four of us would create our own makeshift family, a family of friends. They asked about Bunker and I told them what a mellow puppy he was, how he would love all of them. They all responded with such eager enthusiasm about meeting him that tears crept to my eyes. It was both their openness and kindness, but also their seeming immediate acceptance of me that moved me so deeply. That, and this was my first real afternoon being away from Bunker. I missed him terribly. Not having him next to me left me feeling untethered. I tried not to think about how much time we'd spend apart once I found my first job, which had to happen soon. My bank account was running low.

We said good-bye on the sidewalk outside of the pub and planned our move-in for one week later. Melissa gave me the address of the house they'd found so that I could swing by and check it out. She said it was in Queen Anne, and that it was beautiful. It had a huge yard we could landscape however we wanted, four separate bedrooms, two big bathrooms, and a deck off the kitchen and dining room that had incredible views of downtown Seattle and Mount Rainier. The rent was only $400 per person per month. We'd gotten approved for the property after Chris's mom wrote a letter to the landlord saying what wonderful, upstanding, and responsible young people we were. I asked if it mattered that I didn't have a job yet and Melissa said the landlord had never asked. "Sucker!" she said. "Who cares anyway? We got the place!" I hugged her good-bye and walked to my car, realizing as I drove back to Aunt Aurora's that I was smiling.

Bunker greeted me at the door with his happy dance, his body bending and wiggling wildly. I held his head in my hands, inhaled his beautiful puppy breath, kissed his fur, and whispered, "We're going to be okay, buddy."

1618 Taylor Avenue North

September 1996

The next day my cousin Lindsay and I drove to the Queen Anne neighborhood of Seattle to check out the rental house. Bunker was in the backseat as we drove up a steep hill and pulled up to the place. The house was big, partially hidden behind an enormous pine tree. It was gray with white trim, and the large flowerpots out front held long-dead plants.

We knocked and one of the current tenants let us in, clearly waking up from his midday nap, rubbing his eyes, and going back to bed after telling us to feel free to look around. Lindsay and I laughed quietly, then started snooping. The house was big, drafty, and old, with huge windows and tons of light pouring in. On the first floor was a living room with a large fireplace flanked by built-in bookshelves. The kitchen was small but functional, and the dining room had a huge plate-glass window that looked out over the city. A door from the kitchen led to a deck that wrapped around two sides of the house and offered jaw-dropping views of the Seattle skyline and Mount Rainier.

Left of the living room were two small rooms and a staircase leading to three bedrooms and a second bathroom upstairs. From the kitchen, steps led down to an unfinished basement that held a mustard-yellow pool table and a refrigerator painted with "BEER" in block letters.

Bunker and I wandered out the basement door to what Melissa had assured me would be a great yard for a dog. It was a big, slanted expanse of overgrowth. From the basement door, down a flight of creaky stairs, the yard sloped to a fence buried in vines. Bunker and I made our way down, walked all the way to the edge of the large lot, pushing weeds and branches out of our way.

I stood at the base of the hill and peered up at the house feeling as if I'd been sent to rescue this little patch of land, to reclaim it, care for it, show how resilient the earth can be, even in the most neglected and misused spaces. As I walked, I picked up crushed beer cans and fast-food wrappers. A long snake-like shape that I'm pretty sure was the tail of an enormous rat scurried through the brush. And I thought, *This has potential.*

"We can make this work, buddy. Don't you think?" I said to Bunker, scratching his rump. He looked up at me, his mouth open in a smile before he scurried, deeply focused on the mysterious movement in the grass. I imagined pulling all the weeds, making a real lawn, a vegetable garden even, building a beautiful doghouse out of scrap wood, finding an old patio set and making a little area for outdoor lounging, hanging twinkling lights, and planting flowers.

I wanted to dig my hands into the dirt right there, mark my presence. My cousin called down from the deck off of the living room, "Come check out this view!" Bunker and I began to climb the stairs to join her. On the third step up, Bunker stumbled. His back legs gave out in a flattened splay. He yelped. I gasped and lifted his rear end up and watched concerned as he swayed up the rest of the stairs. I reached the top step and looked back down expecting to find a hole in one of the planks, but saw nothing, so tried not to worry. He must have missed a step or slipped. But in the back of my mind, fear grew. Mom and I had never taken Bunker to the vet after the Sun Valley hike. What if something really was wrong?

Soon we joined Lindsay at the deck's railing and took in the view: Mount Rainier to the left, downtown Seattle to the right, big open sky as far as we could see. The sun pouring over the city made us ignore that when we walked, the deck swayed with the stress of our weight. We smiled, locked eyes, a wordless celebration. I felt welcomed by the energy of this big house, its openness, its light and air, its need. As we thanked the soon-to-vacate tenant and left, I stood on the sidewalk with Bunker and thought about what a contrast this new life would be compared to my dark bedroom in Manhattan. I could plant grass and flowers, sit outside, and feel the sun and rain on my face.

Lindsay was fourteen and I could tell that she thought that my soon-to-be new life was the coolest thing ever. We drove home with the windows down, Pearl Jam blaring, singing at the top of our lungs, the wind whipping our hair into our faces. It was a celebration of new beginnings. As we crossed the bridge over Lake Washington, Bunker stood up in the backseat, looked out at the water and howled, as if to announce our arrival in this beautiful city. I felt like the summer sun would never set on that day.

I thought for a moment about the pot on the stove in my dingy New York apartment, the crawling to the phone, and though it was less than six months earlier, it felt like a lifetime away. Everything before Bunker felt as if it happened in another lifetime. I wasn't awake until I found him, and he found me. Our bond felt that strong, my essence renewed in his presence. He healed me, and to thank him, I planned to give him the best life possible. He was barely six months old, still a puppy. But I looked in the rearview mirror and saw in his sparkling brown eyes an ancient soul, one who came to me with a distinct purpose. I nodded in gratitude to whatever forces brought us together. I reached back with the hand that wasn't on the steering wheel and petted his head. He closed his eyes and leaned into my touch. We were together in this new adventure. I couldn't wait to get started.

We moved into the house a week later, helping each other with our things. Before unpacking, we ordered a celebratory pizza and clinked Red Hook beer bottles on the back deck. The planks wobbled when we walked, and we joked that were it to fall, Chris, who was closest to the house, would grab onto the doorjamb and we'd all grab onto him. It was August in Seattle and the weather was divine: warm sun, cool breeze, and a feeling of contentment and satisfaction that I chalked up to this city. Our conversation felt like one long belly laugh. I knew it already—Seattle and these friends just worked for me. I lay in bed at night those first few weeks thinking that I must have been a Northwestern girl accidentally switched at birth with a bunch of Midwesterners.

My roommates gave me the biggest bedroom in the house, the one on the first floor closest to the front door, and Melissa got the room with the view of Mount Rainier. Greg's room was directly above mine. Somehow Chris landed the bedroom not much wider than a twin bed, but he said he didn't care, that he planned to only sleep there, that's all. His generosity endeared us all to him.

We unpacked, walked the dog, grocery shopped, watched television together, and I gave up on the lingering fear that moving to Seattle could go the way of my horrible year in New York. My housemates already felt like family. Melissa laughed with abandon and confided in me like she already trusted that I would be a good, loyal friend. She'd call me and say only, "Hey, it's me." The way she assumed intimacy between us was an unexpected gift that I wasn't sure I knew how to accept or reciprocate. I wanted desperately to honor her trust in me, so I found myself showing up for her as a friend in ways I never had. I'd always understood that female friendships were special, but I realized in Seattle that I'd never really had a best friend. Soon we were inseparable. We sat hip-to-hip on the couch, laughing about how we didn't care that our asses were expanding as we watched *Sixteen Candles* for the third time on a Sunday at noon in our pajamas. Pass the Ben & Jerry's.

Melissa loved Bunker, and he adored her. She called, "Bunkah, aroooo," when she saw him and he pranced to her, spinning, and finally giving her the howl she asked for. He was our buddy, all of ours, and I felt like a single mom who had moved into a commune that had happily adopted both my child and me.

Bunker loved the roommates, but he snuggled the most with Greg, who worked crazy hours in his laboratory. Many nights, Greg would ride his bike home around midnight, after working a fourteen-hour day. Bunker would stir at the sound of Greg's key in the door and greet him quietly, the last of our makeshift family to return to the den. When Greg grabbed a bag of Goldfish crackers and sat on the couch to watch *SportsCenter*, Bunker would hop up and lie down next to him, resting his chin on Greg's lap, hoping for a dropped fish or two.

Greg moved in with just a mattress, a dresser, a futon, an old television, and a garbage bag full of shoes and clothes. When I asked him what other furniture he had at his apartment, he said mostly he used cardboard boxes for tables and just never spent time there. "My old place was above a futon shop on a loud street," he said. "Crappy place to spend my first year of grad school." I felt a tenderness toward him that felt kind of like a crush, but less urgent. Normally my crushes felt critical—like I had to act on my feelings for that boy instantly, get him before he got away. This was more of a calm admiration, and I sat with it for a few weeks, just enjoying the feeling of having a cute, blue-eyed boy sleeping in the bedroom above mine. I remember listening to his footfalls on the old, creaky floorboards and imagining what it would be like to tiptoe up the stairs and slip into bed next to him.

WORK

SEPTEMBER 1996

I needed a job. I had only about seven hundred dollars left, four hundred of which would go to rent in a few weeks. My one year of experience in publishing in New York didn't help me find connections or a job in Seattle, so I signed up at a local temp agency. My first day of work would be as a receptionist at a law firm. The night before, I lay in bed petrified about how I would fare without Bunker by my side. Leaving Bunker was, for me, like taking someone off of a lifesaving medication and tossing them into a foot race. I dreaded sitting behind a desk all day in an office building. But I woke early, resigned to walk Bunker, then shower, get dressed, and go. I had no choice. I pulled on my long black skirt telling myself that I could do it. The receptionist job was part time, so I would only have to sustain myself without him for about five or six hours.

I walked Bunker in the early dawn, his orange fur glinting in the rising sun. It was a cloudless day, and that seemed a good omen. I talked to him about needing to leave, that I'd be back soon, and he would be okay in his crate. The two consistent things about all of this transition in his young life were his crate and me. He happily trotted in and accepted a treat, and I told him I loved him and would be back as soon as I could. I opened the window a bit so he would have some fresh air, and then I walked out the door.

The longing for him was instantaneous. At the bus stop, I had to talk myself out of running back to the house and locking us in our room, never coming out. When the bus came and I climbed on, I watched my bedroom window disappear slowly as we descended the hill. I looked around and thought that no one on this bus knew the terrible feeling I carried. No one knew how hard it was for me to be away from the one thing that saves me. Did anyone else feel this way? I decided that everyone would deem me insane if I confessed my intense attachment to my dog. The thought left me isolated, lonely inside a world in my head—a very old and familiar place indeed. I felt terrifyingly close to the old Julie who sat on the subway trying to be invisible.

Then an old, frail woman clutching a black pleather purse against her chest smiled at me and said, "Oh, darling. You're beautiful inside. I can see." Her voice was quiet, bird-like. I just about gasped. I thanked her, sat down next to her, and said, "Oh wow. Thank you. You're beautiful too."

With the help of that kind stranger, I made it through the day. The job was fine. The head receptionist wore a bright-red pantsuit and had hair so thickly sprayed that not one strand moved all day. She took me under her wing in a sweet, motherly way. When 1:59 flipped to 2:00 and I was done for the day, despite terrible hunger because I'd forgone lunch, I hopped on the first bus and raced to my door.

"Bunker!" I said, tossing my things on the floor and rushing to the crate. "I'm home!" I sat on the floor and he walked over to me, curling his body into mine, kissing my face. Happy chills coursed up my spine. All of the day's anxieties vanished. "Walk time?" I asked. "Wanna go for a walk?" It was a phrase he knew, and he pranced in circles by the front door. I grabbed a bagel in the kitchen, held it between my teeth as I took off my work clothes and pulled on a pair of sweatpants and a T-shirt. I laced up my tennis shoes and clipped on his leash, and we were off.

Soon we would establish this daily walking route through the neighborhood to Queen Anne Avenue. I was teaching him to diligently stop at all corners and sit down before crossing the street. A few blocks into our walk, we always stopped by the kids' soccer field that doubled as a late-afternoon dog park, and he sniffed and visited with the other dogs. He never really raced around the park, mostly sat down next to me and leaned against my leg. Friendly dog owners commented on how he was glued to my side, and I smiled, said that he was a typical golden retriever, more interested in people than other dogs.

Back at the house that afternoon, Bunker snoozed on the floor while I sat with Melissa, discussing her boyfriend. He'd suddenly begun talking about breaking up. The idea struck her as ludicrous because they both agreed that they were wonderful together. She had fallen deeply in love for the first time, but he told her he wasn't sure she was the one for him. "I just don't get it," she said, wiping the tears that wouldn't stop. "I thought we were so good together. I guess he just doesn't love me." I handed her tissues, sat with her under warm blankets, and listened. I knew her pain, and I wanted to be there for her. I understood that heartbreak felt nearly impossible, that it tore you up in ways you couldn't anticipate. I knew she would go over the same conversations in her mind, that she would pine for him in strange ways, pray for the phone to ring, look for him everywhere. I tried to just listen.

Those early weekends, I worked in the yard. We hadn't been in the rental house a month, and the back yard was already starting to shape up. I had cleared the weeds and picked up the garbage, dug a small switchback pathway and paved it with the bricks and stones that I found buried just under the soil. I built a makeshift doghouse. Bunker and I spent long afternoons knee-deep in dirt and weeds as the other roommates watched from above, every now and then marveling at our progress. I felt mildly self-conscious about my determination to transform the yard, but that quickly faded when I thought about what Bunker needed and what I wanted for him. Besides, sculpting the landscape around me was in my blood. On the afternoons when I walked into the house covered in sweat and bugs, my skin stinging because it'd been sliced and poked by weeds and thorns, I felt a quiet pride because I was indeed my mother's daughter.

Fire and Air

October 1996

One weekend a few months into our lives as housemates, Greg, Chris, and I took my truck out to the Gorge Amphitheater, a postcard-worthy concert venue on the Columbia River, a few hours east of Seattle. Melissa stayed back in Seattle for work and to spend some time with her now ex-boyfriend, to try to make sense of their parting, to somehow manage the end of their relationship gracefully.

At the Gorge, we saw Phish in concert and tailgated in the grass. I didn't know much about Phish, but I liked hanging out with the guys, and my attraction to Greg was intensifying. He was easy to hang out with, funny as hell, and smart. The three of us danced in the grass, drank beer, and took a picture with the Gorge behind us, a deep rock canyon, a backdrop so beautiful it practically seemed fake.

We drove home from the concert across the dark, steep mountains. Chris slept in the backseat and I asked Greg about his astrological sign. "Honestly? I don't know," he said. "I think I'm a Sagittarius." This, the sign most compatible with mine, Libra, seemed to me the official signal that my crush was entering a new and possibly fruitful phase.

"Oh, man," I said, smiling. He smiled too, as if he knew exactly what I meant. But I felt conflicted about disrupting our house's vibe if we were to hook up. We were four young friends living together. So much would change if two of us paired off into a couple, especially as Melissa endured a difficult breakup. A relationship between Greg and me was probably a bad idea. But still, I remember feeling oddly overcome that night, traveling back to our house nestled high on the hill. The road was dark, Chris snored, and I began to fall for Greg. But this felt different than past romances where I was swept away, unable to contain my emotion. This wasn't a lightning bolt. I didn't swoon. I just thought, calmly, "I could really love this man."

In October, my mom and dad arrived for a three-day visit around my birthday. I'd been in the new house only about six weeks and the visit seemed too soon, but it also seemed belated. Their encouragement and enthusiasm were a salve. I was already doing well, but their delight at how things had turned made me think I'd managed a miraculous recovery. The question was whether it would last.

At dinner in the city, they asked about the depression and whether it was threatening any kind of return. I didn't have an answer for them. How was I supposed to know? I didn't know it was coming the first time I collapsed. I felt okay so far. Wasn't that enough? These kinds of conversations left me feeling as if I were walking a tightrope. One glance in the wrong direction, one wrong thought, and I'd slip, entangle myself in the line, and fall into the abyss.

The first night my parents were in town, Greg was out with his lab-mates having a few beers. My parents were asleep in my bed, so I was relegated to the futon in the living room. I was half-awake in the pitch dark when the front door opened and Greg walked in. The streetlamp's light flooded the entryway and Bunker rose to greet him, tail wagging, breathing heavily. Greg leaned down to pet him. "Hi, buddy," he said. "Sorry. Didn't mean to wake you, bud." He closed the door and tiptoed by the futon. I opened my eyes and smiled at him. "Did I wake you up?" he asked.

"No, I was just daydreaming," I said.

"Pre-dreaming," he whispered. "Planning what you'll dream

about after you fall asleep." He sat down on the edge of the futon and pulled off his backpack. "Never too early to prepare," he said, smiling.

"Have a fun night?" I asked stretching my arms above my head. He said that they'd gone to Big Time, his favorite bar near campus, and then he stopped talking. He just looked at me. I wondered if he felt the connection too, then he leaned down, held my face in his hands, and kissed me. For a moment I thought about my parents lying in the next room, but that reality slipped away with the kiss, with the weight of his body soon on top of mine. I remember thinking that he was more *man* than I'd ever felt, his broad shoulders and sure arms. I arched my back into his kiss. We made out for a while, until he finally pulled himself away. "Don't want to be caught here in the morning by your parents," he whispered, laughing.

"Yeah," I said. "No doubt."

"See you in the morning," he said. He kissed me again, stood up, and started toward the stairs. "Man, I've been waiting a long time to do that." He laughed, did a little fist pump, and headed up to his bedroom.

I did a giddy little twist on the futon and held my hands to my mouth. *He'd been waiting a long time to do that.* That was one of the nicest things anyone had ever said to me.

My parents, Aunt Aurora and I spent the next day at my new favorite dog park, a place east of Seattle called Marymoor. My aunt and cousins had taken me there with Bunker and their dog Brandy. I watched as Bunker flung himself into the Sammamish River after sticks and balls, then dripped through the woods following a scent. Bunker absolutely loved the water. Swimming was his bliss. When Bunker was happy, I was happy. My dad and I walked behind him on a quiet trail. We were a few paces ahead of everyone else. "Man," my dad said, "Bunker just *loves* this place."

"I know," I said. "I try to come here at least once a week. It's his favorite place for sure."

"And you?" my dad asked. "You're still happy?"

I walked a few more paces, smiled, kicked a few leaves, and said, "Yep." I thought of Greg's kiss the night before, of my easy job that paid the bills just fine, my daily, curative walks with Bunker. I thought about writing more, about how I would look for an editing job, but felt no pressure just yet. I thought about Melissa and Chris and Greg and our house, how we would get a keg and call our friends and invite everyone over for pizza and beer. How when a friend fell asleep on the pool table, we laughed and took pictures after sticking Goldfish crackers up his nose.

"I'm really, really good, Dad. Seattle really fits me well."

My dad put his arm around my shoulder and squeezed me tight. He kissed the top of my head and said, "I'm so happy, Julie." His voice cracked. "I'm so happy for you."

Bunker ran ahead of us, then tripped and his back legs gave out behind him like they'd suffered instant paralysis. He whimpered and yelped, then fell down screaming a nearly human cry of pain. I ran to him. My dad started running too, and soon we were kneeling over Bunker, our hands hovering over him, not sure whether we should touch him. He was lying on his side wagging his tail, panting.

"What the hell happened?" my dad said.

"I have no idea. He just kind of fell." I gently touched his back, his hips, his hind legs, and Bunker just lay there panting and smiling at us. My mom and Aunt Aurora caught up with us. Aurora said, "Was that scream from *Bunker*?"

She knelt down and whispered calmly to him, "Shhh. Shhh. It's okay, buddy. Something hurts, huh?" She looked at me with alarm. I could see that she wanted to say something but thought better of it. I imagined the worst. Bone cancer. Doggie leukemia.

"What?" I asked. "What do you think is wrong?"

"I don't know," Aurora said, sounding too chipper for the face she'd just made. "Must've stepped in a hole or something. Twisted his leg. Let's see if we can get him up." She instructed me to stand next to him, then she walked ahead a bit and called him to her. He wouldn't get up. "You switch with me. I'll catch him if he falls. You call him to you."

My hands were shaking. "Bunker," I said, backing away from him slowly. "Come here, buddy. Can you get up? Come on, let's get you back to the car." Brandy swooped by me and Bunker watched him sprint along to the creek's edge. "Come on, buddy." Bunker panted and then stood up and walked toward me shakily.

"See?" Aurora said unconvincingly. "He looks okay."

Bunker limped right next to me the rest of the hike. He didn't romp. He didn't play. He did not walk like a seven-month-old puppy but rather like a geriatric dog that couldn't manage exertion. I saw Aurora whisper to my mom. I imagined the worst, and Bunker stayed right by my side.

My parents left the next morning. I promised I would take Bunker to the veterinarian, but the idea left me paralyzed with dread.

As I prepared to drive my parents to the airport the next morning, Bunker seemed fine again. He hopped into the car without any hesitation. The worry wouldn't leave me, though. My mom sat in the backseat with him and mentioned that I might want to take him to the vet just to be sure, but not to worry because he probably just slipped.

I nodded, not wanting to think about it. The whole idea of something being wrong with Bunker was too terrifying. So I told them that I was thinking about dating Greg. I watched as my dad tried to hide his delight. "He seems cool," he said, before he not-so-covertly winked at my mom. They approved.

Blossoming
November 1996

Greg and I were proceeding slowly in our secret relationship. For much of those fall months, soon after everyone in the house went to bed, Greg would drift down the stairs to my room, or I'd go to his. I remember tiptoeing up the stairs, cursing the loose floorboards and squeaking door hinges. We didn't want Melissa or Chris to know that we were fooling around. Our pairing off would forever change our house's wonderful energy.

Bunker hadn't fallen again, or shown any sign of distress, so I put off taking him to the veterinarian. He climbed gingerly up the steps with me at night as if he knew he had to be quiet. When we reached Greg's room, often Greg would be in bed reading and once he saw me, he would put the papers down and take me in his arms. Bunker would lie on the floor and fall asleep quietly. Greg and I talked in whispers as we grew to know one another. Greg's wit was quick, and it was difficult not to laugh out loud. Soon we'd begin kissing, petting, and slowly pulling off each other's clothes. Sometimes we would hear Chris or Melissa heading to the bathroom and we would freeze, desire building in us because all of this was a secret, and a little bit forbidden.

I couldn't deny that when I felt the weight of Greg's body at the edge of my bed, from a deep sleep, my arms would instinctively reach out for him like they realized they desperately needed him the exact moment he appeared. My eyes would stay closed, and we would move together, our mouths on each other's necks, our breathing deep, calm. We'd kiss slowly, exploring, quietly, even innocently. Nothing below the waist; I'd asked for that. He respected my request, and I wondered if he wanted me only because he couldn't entirely have me. But then I'd feel his hands, his soft and silken, callous-free hands, the hands of an intellectual, a thinker. Something about the softness of them made me trust that this man was different. I remember thinking: *I can love a kind man.* This thought came as a revelation.

We didn't talk about what we did at night. Then Greg would brush his finger on my hip as he passed me in the kitchen. That touch would send a firecracker through me. But part of me held back. It seemed too soon to have a new boyfriend. Since I was eighteen, I'd been in relationships all but a few months. It was comfortable to have a boyfriend, but for the first time, I craved independence. The few months of single life in Seattle had suited me surprisingly well. Greg commented that my autonomy was something he admired. We had fun together, laughed, made out, and talked for hours. This was not an all-encompassing kind of love. It was easy and fun, not desperate like the love I'd known with Will and Brian. That kind of love meant crazy longing and inevitable emotional distress. It meant crippling fear of losing something that sustained me. Now I felt fine if Greg and I didn't connect for a while. I didn't long for his call or get frustrated if he didn't come to see me in the dark of night for a few days. I wondered if this meant that I wasn't really that interested in him. I felt great with him, but I also felt great without him. Maintaining my autonomy didn't feel like the kind of love I'd always known, so I second-guessed our connection. It was easy. He was easy. He was calm and fun and didn't act like he owned me. He was interested in me, and liked me, clearly, but he didn't expect me to want to be with him every second. He didn't mind if another guy called the house asking to talk to me, even Will. He encouraged Melissa and me to go out on our own. "Have fun," he'd say, and he'd mean it. "Have a great time."

Melissa and I had a blast out on the town in Seattle. We would go see our favorite band, The Super Sonic Soul Pimps, and we'd dance in the mosh pit and try to figure out how we could approach the adorable bass player. One night she stayed out late, but I was tired so I took the bus back up the hill and returned to an empty house. Greg was still working and Chris was out with friends.

I snuggled with Bunker alone, then picked up the phone and called Will. We still talked. Truth was, when it came to Will, the man who didn't show up when I needed him, I couldn't get enough. He told me that leaving me was the worst mistake of his life. I wanted to hear him say this a thousand times. I inhaled his sorrow and regret. I wanted to believe that none of the men in my life had ever meant to hurt me. I wanted my father to tell me that he wished he'd been home more, not working so much and missing everything. I wanted to believe that Clay would come to me some-day and say that he didn't know what he was thinking when he chased me, hit me, insulted me. I wanted him to explain, over and over and over, that it had absolutely nothing to do with me, that I was okay, that he actually liked me.

Blizzard in Seattle

December 1996

Melissa was still suffering through her breakup and had gone home for an extended Christmas break. She'd asked me to pick her up at the airport on the 30th of December, and I put it on my calendar. I was working that Monday. I'd been hired full time as a receptionist at a small downtown law firm. Soon after I started at the job, a very handsome bike messenger started appearing at my desk almost daily. He was everything I'd fallen for in the past: rugged, handsome, tall, rough around the edges, and nothing but trouble. His name was Glenn, and he asked me out on a date. I accepted. No one ever had to know. I could just see how it went. Greg and I hadn't had sex yet, hadn't discussed our relationship status. I could go on one measly date.

That day, forecasters were calling for an enormous snowstorm. Routes across the Cascades were closed, weathermen warned of several feet of snow falling, then a warming that would turn the snow into slushy rivers pouring down city streets. At work, everyone was talking about the storm, how offices would most likely be closed on Tuesday. But I wasn't really paying attention because I was looking forward to my secret date with a brand-new bad boy.

We went to a bar in Belltown, had a few beers, and talked to the bartenders about the coming weather. Glenn was fit and attractive with dark hair and a wry, mischievous smile. But he only wanted to talk about his motorcycle and a new tattoo he planned to ink the next weekend. I deduced, based on the complete lack of information he offered about his personal life, that he probably had a girlfriend or maybe even a wife. We watched the snow come down outside the bar window, marveling at the beauty of it, chain-smoking cigarettes like morons. Soon Glenn said, "I live pretty far outside the city. Maybe I should crash at your place tonight since you're right in Queen Anne."

I knew exactly what he was suggesting. I grinned, a bit giddy from the nicotine. "Oh, yes. Definitely a much safer option." I blew smoke out of the corner of my mouth, all kinds of emotion rushing inside of me. Part of me did not want him to come to my house, but I had no idea how to tell a man "No." I didn't want to hurt his feelings or make him sad, because I didn't want him to hurt *my* feelings or make *me* sad.

"Can we get the tab?" Glenn asked, his eyes still fixed on mine.

We took the bus back to the Taylor house, locked my bedroom door, and dove into bed. I didn't even know if I wanted to do it, but I did. I'd never had a one-night stand. The momentary ecstasy with Glenn was followed, of course, by terrible guilt and instant regret. Lying naked next to Glenn late that night, I heard Greg climb the outside stairs to the house, enter, go to the kitchen, then to my door. Clear as day, I realized: I had sabotaged this good thing with Greg. It was too healthy, too easy. It was midnight and he'd been working since nine that morning. He knocked lightly, so as not to wake Chris upstairs. Melissa wasn't home; she was flying back to Seattle from Ohio and I was supposed to pick her up at the airport, but I assumed her flight was cancelled due to the storm.

Instead I lay naked next to a man I didn't care about, who didn't care about me. Glenn slept soundly while I had visions of tossing him out the window, pushing him out onto the sidewalk. Greg knocked again and Bunker stirred. He looked at me as if to say, *Now you've really blown it.*

I closed my eyes, took a deep breath, ignored Greg's third knock, and planned my lie: that I slept through his knocks, that I was sick, that I fell asleep with headphones on. It came as a sickly realization that Greg must've known I wasn't alone because Glenn's souped-up bike leaned against the mantle in the living room.

Soon I heard slow footsteps ascend the stairs and I put my face in my hands. Greg's mattress creaked above as he climbed into bed alone, and I longed to leave Glenn, tiptoe up the steps, and slip into bed next to the kind, beautiful man who I knew would treat me well. What had I done? I imagined leaving a note for Glenn asking him to please leave upon waking, to just disappear. But I was locked under Glenn's muscled arm, unable to move—not because I physically couldn't, but because I was afraid. Part of me wanted this: wild sex with Glenn, a man I knew would hurt me, leave me, and treat me terribly. This was what I knew. This was comfortable, familiar. I was helpless to the pull of a man who might not love me. I lay in bed thinking: *Idiot. You deserve assholes because you're an asshole.*

The phone rang at midnight and I heard Melissa's voice on the answering machine through the wall. She'd made it to Seattle but was stranded at the airport in the snowstorm. I lay there frozen, sinking even further. *Fuck, fuck, fuck.* I pulled open the blinds and the snow was coming down hard now, at least six inches on the ground. A bus skidded down Taylor Avenue, braking erratically to try to slow itself down, nearly sideswiping my truck. Melissa's voice was pleading on the answering machine, "Are you coming to get me? There are, like, no cabs or anything. We're completely snowed in and you're the only one I know with four-wheel drive. Can you please come and get me? Hello? What's going on?"

It's indefensible, all of this, but I did it. I screwed around and ruined a sweet, budding romance. I stranded my best friend at the airport. I didn't even get up to answer her call. I stayed in bed under a strange man's strong arm and, at the time, I didn't know why. I was comfortable being trapped under him, content to suffer in the familiar territory of a man who didn't care about me. I couldn't accept kindness from a man; it honestly repulsed me. I didn't trust that I could be the kind of friend Melissa deserved, the good friend she thought I was. I only knew that I'd just completely betrayed the two most important people in my life. I was a statue that had once come alive, then turned back into stone.

When I woke in the morning, Bunker was sitting up, looking at me as if to say, *Who's this guy? Where's the nice-smelling guy?* He jumped on the bed and stepped on both of us. It's worth noting that Bunker *never* jumped on the bed and stepped on me. Glenn laughed, "Whoa!" he said, too loud, protecting his naked penis from Bunker's sharp claws. "Hey, buddy! Nice to see you too!"

I slipped out from under Glenn's arm and put my underwear on. Glenn's sexy ruggedness from the night before appeared pock-marked and scarred in the morning. He asked if he could smoke in my room and I mumbled that the landlord didn't allow it.

How would I get Glenn out without Greg seeing? I couldn't tell Glenn that I was sort of dating someone else, and I couldn't let Greg see Glenn. They would both hate me. I stopped dead, said nothing, and Glenn dressed as I sat on the edge of my bed in dirty jeans, a T-shirt, and no bra.

"That was awesome, baby," he said, holding the back of my neck and kissing me again. I smiled awkwardly and we clanked teeth. "I gotta get back on the bike, get home, and clean up before another day of dodging dumbass Seattle drivers—in snow, no less. See you later?"

"Sounds good," I said, tempted to ask him to leave through the window. He pulled his messenger bag across his chest and walked out of my room. I heard the click-click-click of his bike chain in the living room. "Hey, man," he said, to someone. I held my hand to my mouth, praying that it was Chris who saw Glenn. I sat on my bed and prayed that Melissa had made it home safely. I prayed that Greg might forgive me. I prayed that I hadn't fucked up my new life.

I watched out my window as Glenn rolled his bike onto the sidewalk, hopped on, and slid carelessly down slushy Queen Anne Hill. Bunker whined to go outside. I had no choice but to face my newest mess; Bunker's bladder wouldn't let me hide in my room all day. I cracked open my bedroom door, pulled it with a slow creak, and Bunker trotted out and turned the corner into the living room. I heard Greg's voice whisper, heavy with sadness, "Hey, buddy."

I wanted to scream. What would I say? How would I explain what I'd done? How could I say how stupid I was? That I knew I had just ruined this beautiful, sweet connection we were cultivating? That I didn't know what drove me to do it? That I was self-destructive and maybe it was best that he not date me?

I stepped into the room, struck with one glance by the heartbreak etched on Greg's face. He looked at me, searchingly, as if trying to understand who I was after all. I opened my mouth to speak but he shook his head, got up, and walked away. He went upstairs and slammed the door, and I stood in the living room with my hand on my stomach, sour juices flowing. If I had to choose between Greg and Glenn, I would choose Greg a million times over—no question. But something about his kindness, his ease, made him less attractive to me. I understood men like Glenn: men who left, men who didn't show up, men who knew that I was not worthy, men who had more important things to do with their time, who thought they could do better than dumb, ugly me.

After Bunker went outside to pee, I sat in the living room in my pajamas. When Greg came downstairs, I tried to speak, but he left without a word. He walked out the door, got into his blue Ford Taurus with nearly bald tires that slid like sleds in the snow, and swerved up over the hill toward campus. He left without even looking at me.

Bunker came to me and sat at my feet, leaning into me, bringing undeserved relief to my newest fuck-up. I kissed his soft head, petted his little skull bump, and whispered a quiet *Shhhhit*. Part of me wanted to call Glenn, ask for a nooner. Get drunk at 2 p.m. and run through the snowy streets acting idiotic. But Bunker lay down and groaned, and I stayed with him. I sat down on the floor next to him and took a few long, deep breaths, watching the clouds multiply over Lake Union. I didn't call Glenn. I didn't do anything. I just sat in silence and soon began to contemplate that perhaps what I needed was to be alone. I didn't need Glenn or Will or Greg. I just needed my dog.

Two Bad Options

January 1997

At the stroke of midnight on New Year's Eve 1997, I was lying on the couch in the house in the darkened living room, praying. Greg and Chris had gone out to celebrate. Greg wasn't talking to me and we'd managed to avoid each other since the night of the blizzard. The roommates didn't know what was going on between us, and not talking to anyone about it compounded my confusion. Melissa came downstairs the morning after I'd failed to pick her up at the airport, walked past me, got a cup of coffee, then returned. She sat down across from me and said, "What the fuck happened? Where were you?" I had no defendable answer, so I just said, "I'm so, so sorry. I'm so sorry. I was sure your flight was cancelled. I've just fucked everything up." She agreed and said she'd been really disappointed. She was still suffering through her breakup, and I had literally abandoned her in a storm. I couldn't tell her what was going on, that I'd probably just ruined the best chance I'd ever had at a healthy relationship. She hugged me, clearly sensing my distress, and told me it was okay. I knew it wasn't, though. I knew I'd betrayed her trust.

In the aftermath of the terrible storm, Melissa and I decided to stay home for New Year's Eve, wear pajamas, and watch TV. When the clock struck twelve, she was on the deck watching the celebration over the Space Needle. "Come see the fireworks!" she shouted through the kitchen door. "They're beautiful!"

"Okay, just a minute," I said. Before I got up, I clasped my hands together in front of my mouth, closed my eyes, and whispered,

"Please let Bunker be okay. Please let him be okay. Please." Bunker was having trouble climbing stairs, so I finally scheduled the vet appointment for January 2. I prayed that the veterinarian would say that Bunker was just a clumsy puppy, that he'd grow out of these scary falls. I prayed that I would figure out what had motivated me to treat such a lovely man with such disrespect. I prayed that I would be a better friend to Melissa.

I took a deep breath and joined Melissa on the deck. The fireworks were beautiful, but the noise scared Bunker, so I told Melissa I was going to watch from inside the house. With each burst of light and color, a new possible diagnosis raged through my mind: bone disease, hip dysplasia, leukemia, cancer. I sat down on the floor next to Bunker, feeling his back, pushing on his hind legs to see if he'd respond. Nothing. He was terrified of the loud booming and pushed his nose into my lap. I held him, put my head on his back, saying, "Shhh. I got you, boy. I got you. It's okay." I listened to the strong beat of his heart.

He'd been neutered a few weeks earlier. I felt such confidence during the day of his surgery. The morning I dropped him off for the procedure, I drove to work feeling completely unworried. When I paused to examine that confidence, I decided it stemmed from a deep, abiding knowledge that Bunker was sent to me, that he was my comfort, and for him to leave me this soon wouldn't make sense.

But that New Year's Day night, before the next day's appointment, I tried and failed to stop myself from falling into catastrophic thinking. Bunker lay on the bed with me, his back curved into my belly. I opened my bedroom window to see if I could see the moon. Nothing. Just clouds. The only thing that helped was remembering that I would do whatever it took to make sure he was healthy. Anything. I held his body, calmed by the rise and fall of his chest. I finally fell asleep with my face pressed to the soft red fur at the back of his head.

When I woke in the morning, he was sitting on the floor next to the bed, watching me like I was a present he had just unwrapped.

I chuckled sleepily, rolled over, and turned off my buzzing alarm. He stood up and wagged his tail like a helicopter about to lift off. "You doofus," I said. "You have me so worried." He backed up, prancing, as I got up out of bed. We went to the back yard and admired our half-done landscaping job. He had no problem with the stairs on the way back into the house. I told myself to relax.

I half-assed my way through work and rushed home to take him to the vet. In the waiting room, I filled out the necessary paperwork, and Bunker sat leaning into my legs. The receptionist smiled at him and said, "Only seven months? So calm!"

I smiled and held him close to my legs, stroked him to settle my own nerves. The vet tech called us in, weighed Bunker, and said he was fifty pounds now.

"So what brings you to see us today?" she asked.

"His back legs keep failing him," I said.

"Oh, no," she said. I couldn't look at her and keep the tears from coming, so I just smiled and watched the floor. My palms went clammy as we waited to see the doctor. "Okay, sweet little guy," she petted the top of his head and he opened his mouth into a smile. "We'll send the doctor right in." She left and I wrapped my arms around Bunker's chest. I was keenly aware that I needed his touch right now. This worry was threatening to toss me backwards into a black hole of sorrow.

When the veterinarian came in, he furrowed his brow, his white lab coat crunching as he crossed his arms and listened while I explained the froggy legs on stairs, the yelping. He examined Bunker and his face seemed to darken. Each move the doctor made sent a dose of fear through me. He asked about whether Bunker ran with all four paws or if he "bunny hopped," running with the front two legs staggered and the back two legs together in one motion. This, he said, was a sure sign of weakness in the hind legs. This, I knew, was exactly how my puppy ran.

The vet asked if he could take Bunker to the back for "just a few quick X-rays." I nodded, then sat alone with Bunk's empty leash, feeling like a helium balloon that had just been let go. The longer he was gone, the less oxygen there was in the room.

The technician brought Bunker back and told me that the doctor was going to read the films. "He'll be back in a few minutes, okay?" she said, her tone consoling and sad.

I sat down on the floor, not caring how much dog shit and cat piss might have once sat in that spot. I wanted to be on the ground with my boy, feeling him, holding him, *with* him, as close to the earth as possible. I felt lightheaded and spacey when the door clicked and the veterinarian returned. I awkwardly scrambled to my feet. He paused, indicating with his silence that most pet owners don't sit on the floor of the examination room. The veterinarian stood over me like a big brother and cleared his throat.

"I'm afraid I have some bad news," he said, and his voice began a long descent through a tunnel of sound, as if the tubes in my ears had distended and bent and couldn't take in his words. *Really the worst case I've ever... Not even in the socket. I don't know how he manages to walk. Severe hip dysplasia. Only two options here. Put him down. Probably your most humane. Surgery is very, very painful. Difficult... Cost... Run you about four thousand dollars... recovery... carry to urinate... not sure what you... so sorry... We euthanize here at the office... won't be able to walk for much longer. Save these X-rays for colleagues... Just amazing to see a case this severe... hip socket... complete misalignment.*

I felt stoned. I thought of Clay chasing me down the hallway. That same vein of adrenaline, reserved only for trauma, opened up and ran through my body—only I was older now, stronger. I looked at the vet through squinted eyes.

"We'll do the surgery," I said.

He began speaking, and again I fell backward into the tunnel of this man's voice: *Several thousand dollars... triple pelvic osteotomy... months of recovery... sequester in a crate... break the pelvic bone in six places. Two separate surgeries. Long months of pain for him... Really the most humane option is...*

"Thank you," I said. "But if you mention euthanizing him one more time, I am going to scream bloody fucking murder." My whole body shook. I thought of mothers who could lift cars off of their children. I thought of fathers rushing into burning buildings. The doctor's face registered shock and insult. I didn't care. I wanted to call my mom and scream and cry. I imagined collapsing on the floor of the vet office, Greg rushing to my rescue. Instead, out of my mouth came, "Who's the best hip dysplasia surgeon in Seattle? I want a consultation with him immediately. Where can I do more research? I don't care the cost." In an instant, I was my father, snapping-to in a crisis. I knew how to do this. I knew how to come to someone's rescue. And whether or not this white-coated guy cared, I was going to save my dog.

I drove home, my eyes flooded with tears. The road blurred. Bunker sat in the passenger seat, his back legs splayed in what struck me as a misleadingly comfortable bearing. At a stoplight, I wiped my face and pressed my hand against my chest, trying to collect myself. I held Bunk's shoulder and felt my breath steadying. Just one touch on his body helped me slow down, collect myself. My upper lip buzzed with emotion and I drove the rest of the way home with one arm wrapped around him. The word *euthanasia* would not stop looping through my mind. Bunker leaned down, sniffed my forearm, and licked it with a warm, slow pull of his tongue.

When I reached the house, I parked the car and cut the engine. Bunker was getting tall enough that his head was level with mine when he sat up in the passenger seat. I was panicking. The depression seemed to be threatening a return, like it was sitting in the backseat with a smirk and a knife. It would take out Bunker first, then kill me once and for all.

But when I slowed down, took inventory of how I felt, instead of being defeated or scared or sad, I was furious. I wasn't broken this time. Though the depression seemed closer than ever since Bunker had first come to me, I felt capable of tamping it down, of facing the situation and saving my boy. I wasn't broken; my dearest companion was. This situation uncorked a reserve of strength that I didn't know I had.

It occurred to me, sitting in the driver's seat, one hand on Bunker, one hand on the steering wheel, that perhaps it wasn't just Bunker who had come to save me. Perhaps we had found each other so that I could save him too. The veterinarian had said something about several thousand dollars. He kept repeating euthanasia as the best option, and that many owners choose to put down their dogs, and he bore no ill will toward them. Most people, he said, balked at the price. The veterinarian didn't know that I would've gone into lifelong debt and homelessness to save Bunker. I would've crafted a wheelchair out of sticks and rubble just to keep him alive and with me.

Parked in front of the house, I petted his soft-as-silk ears and said, "We're a pile of broken parts, aren't we, Bunk? We'll fix it." He opened his mouth, panted, blew his warm puppy breath in my face. His breath had become my favorite scent. I was officially a goner. I inhaled, knowing logically that Bunker had no idea what I was saying or what had just happened or what pain and suffering lay ahead for him. But part of me, that same deep-down part that had, since childhood, communed with trees and deer and birds, stirred when I held his head in my hands. I knew that our connection was not of this world, and that my determination and his pure goodness might just conquer any malady either of us suffered.

As Much As a Used Car

I found the best veterinary orthopedic surgeon in Seattle and scheduled an appointment for the next day. There, I gently petted Bunker while the doctor reviewed the X-rays. I had come straight to the clinic after racing home after work. Bunker howled with excitement when I walked inside, led him to the car, and drove off.

Greg still wasn't talking to me, and I wasn't forcing it. I wanted to give him space, and I needed time to consider what I wanted. Glenn blew me off the next time he delivered a package to my office. "That was fun, huh?" he said. "Just a fun night is all." I got the message loud and clear and sat down at the reception desk with a clawing emptiness in my gut.

Sitting on the cold table at the vet's office, Bunker's disappointment was palpable. This was no romp in the park; this was more poking and prodding from a stranger. Bunker was tolerant as the veterinarian pushed and pulled on his legs, pressed his back, and tested his range of movement. As he manipulated Bunker's hips, he made "hmm" sounds, and a few times said quietly, "Okay, all right." This doctor was in his fifties, fit, with a salt-and-pepper beard and hair, and he acted more like a doctor for humans than animals. I wondered if he had an older brother who was an MD, who teased him for doctoring less-important beings. I appreciated his demeanor, his furrowed brow, his sensitivity to my boy's condition.

He began speaking, and after his first few words I lost focus. My hearing muddled again, like I was underwater. This was bad. I saw his frown, his concerned brow, his crossed arms creasing his white coat with the blue cursive letters spelling Dr. So & So in fanciful font that looked too old-fashioned for someone who was saying that our only hope lay in two drastic, highly technical surgeries. Six weeks apart, two complete triple-pelvic-osteotomies. "Repeat that?" I asked. I wanted to know the term. I wanted to brand it into my brain, the fix for this problem: Triple. Pelvic. Os-te-ot-o-my.

"Without the surgery, I'm afraid Dr. Vance is right. He will be immobile before he's two years old. I'm sorry," he said, rubbing his chin, leaving the skin pinkened under his spiky silver goatee.

What did this veterinarian see when he looked at me? A young nervous girl? Could he see my panic, the lump in my throat rising as the situation began to feel more and more dire? Did he feel anything for us? Could he understand just by smelling, or feeling with his sixth doctor sense, the immensity of this situation?

I wanted to tell him that this animal was my lifeline. Without him, I would be confined to an emotional prison cell. I would never know how to lift myself out of the blackness again. I was hurling these thoughts across the room, as if they might enter his ear canal and worm their way to his sympathetic brain center. *Please, please, please, please help me. Please don't make this happen. Dear man, please save my dog.*

"... shave his entire backside. Two plates and six screws, some quite long, inserted into the center of the hipbone, which has been sawed apart into three sections. Then the bone heals in a whole new shape. But the immobility is essential and the healing process is extremely arduous." He actually used the word *saw*, as in chainsaw. I nodded, my brain a fuzz of static. I searched for consolation and failed, like this were a pitch-black room with the light switch installed on the ceiling. I tried my best to listen from the darkness.

I gasped when the vet told me what I should've anticipated, that each surgery would cost over two thousand dollars. I began nearly chanting it in my mind. *Four thousand dollars.* I had less than four hundred in my bank account. I'd just paid my third month's rent and was feeling flush with more than a hundred bucks sitting around. Where the hell was I going to come up with that kind of cash? I couldn't possibly ask my parents for more money. I didn't want to need my parents anymore. I wanted to survive on my own, and I had, so far, succeeded. But with the price tag on this turn of events, here I was, once again, desperately needing outside help.

Out in the parking lot, I stood and blinked, perhaps hoping I would wake from this nightmare. The dim, cloudy light slowly pulled me back into the moment. There would be no waking up from this. Behind my truck, I knelt down next to Bunker, his sweet, happy energy a contrast from the surgeon's office. I tried to remember what the vet said. There was hope that Bunker could be healed. It would be arduous, painful, and difficult to witness. Each surgery would last at least five hours, and Bunker would have to be confined to a crate almost twenty hours a day for eight weeks, carried up and down stairs.

The vet said he would want to walk soon after the surgery. His mind would be ready, but his body wouldn't. I sat listening, distinctly aware of the parallel between this prognosis and mine. I could move someplace new, convince myself that I was better, but my broken spirit still wasn't healed. I still made terrible mistakes, hurt kind people, acted stupidly and self-destructively. There was an internal cascading then, a falling out or down or through, and I turned inward. I would heal Bunker, I promised. And maybe if I just focused on helping him, I could stop hurting everyone else.

New Family, True Friend

February 1997

I called my mom, who was aware of the potential diagnosis, and after her usual singsong hello, came the avalanche of my distress. "Mom," I said, "that vet was right. This one said the same thing. They said Bunker's so malformed that he won't be able to walk in a year if we don't do something." She took a sharp intake of breath and then was silent. My shock became hers, and her quiet felt collusive. This was bad. Really bad. Not what we had planned at all. She quietly asked what I wanted to do, and I told her that there was only the option of surgery. That was all. No other. I didn't mention the price tag, and I made an excuse to get off the phone. I knew she was worried about Bunker, but I also knew she worried that I would become depressed again.

As was my habit, I went to my room, closed the door, and cried. I imagined ways to escape and avoid, moment by moment, these terrible fears. I listened to music, tried to sleep, ate a box of chocolate chip cookies, and watched out the window as cars, buses, and people went by, their lives far better than mine. I was the only one so lost and scared and confused. I was the only one who needed a dog to survive. Clay would laugh at me if he knew.

My sense of isolation was all-encompassing. I still couldn't fully recognize that I had control over my thoughts, that if I were able to see the negative self-talk, I could choose something else. I would not notice that I had a choice whether I told myself, time and again, that I was the only one this weird, this wrong, this weak. I was the only one I knew who was unstable enough to need psychiatric intervention. I hadn't found a therapist in Seattle yet, but I knew that I needed one. I promised myself I would call Aurora and ask for a recommendation. I stayed in my room hiding until late into that night. Dark, quiet corners were best. I curled up there, feeling safe alone. Bunker seemed weak now too, settling in right beside me.

Melissa came home from work late, and I stayed in my bedroom. She wasn't mad anymore about my not showing up for her at the airport. I told her about Glenn, that I'd had raunchy sex with him and felt awful about it. She put together that the night of my one-night stand was also the night I abandoned her at the airport. Her frustration created a distance between us that was real enough that it broke my heart a little, set off the negative voices in my head: *You're such a shitty friend. No wonder you've never had a best friend until now. And look how you treat her.*

I stayed in my room, reeling from the surgeon's concurrent diagnoses. Bunker and I lay on the bed together. From the ceiling, we must've looked like two halves of a heart. His hind legs were curled into his stomach, his front paws resting on my chest. His head curled into my neck, my nose on his forehead. When he stretched and his eyes met mine, I imagined he felt sorry. He was hurting, and he needed me. He knew that I needed him too, but he was not able to do his important work. In his few short months of life, he'd been pure happiness and goodness. How could pain sprout in his body? I cried and imagined that all the pain and blackness Bunker took out of me was finally showing up in him.

Then there was a knock on the door. I stopped my weeping and sat up, whispering, "Shit, shit, shit." Bunker hopped to the floor and stretched, wagging his tail. I snatched a tissue and wiped my face, wishing I'd locked the door as it opened slowly. I could see Melissa's hand, her long, elegant fingers and pretty fingernails, way healthier than my gnawed nubs. She looked at me and I held my breath, trying my very best to look okay, but she saw right through that effort, and I burst into a sob.

None of the roommates knew the extent of my terrible year in New York, of my breakdown or my diagnosis, and I wanted to keep it that way. I wasn't a depressed or sick person to them. I wasn't someone who ruined friendships and didn't show up and cried too often. Before Glenn, I'd reinvented myself in Seattle as someone fun, responsible, thoughtful, and smart. But I felt like I was tricking all of them and now the façade of a put-together person was cracking, and they'd see who I really was: a terrible person, a royal fuck-up, a crazy-dog-lady who believed that if her dog died, she would too.

I couldn't hold in the sobs. "Honey!" Melissa said. She closed the door quietly behind her and came and sat down on the bed next to me. "What's wrong? What happened?" What was remarkable about this moment was that, in her voice, there was no trace of *What's wrong with you?* There was an absence of judgment.

"Bunker's sick," I fumbled. "Well, he's not really sick. He's broken." My voice cracked and I burst into another mucky sob. I hated how familiar this felt. But Melissa sat with me, quietly, peacefully, not yet tired of my tears.

"What do you mean, broken?" she asked, and when I looked at her, I saw tears in her eyes, too. Amidst the avalanche of relief that came at this sight, I leaned across the bed and hugged her and we cried together. We sank down to the floor and sat on either side of Bunker, our hands stroking his resting body. I told her about his hip dysplasia, how severe it was, how it explained why he couldn't climb stairs sometimes. Tears dripped down her cheeks and she petted Bunker's ribs, still soft with silky red puppy fur.

"So what do we do?" she asked, and in that moment I felt, for the first time in my life, that I really did have a real best friend. She could've said, "So what are *you* going to do?" but she didn't. She said "we."

I didn't have the words then to say what this meant to me, how much gratitude I felt that she intended to fight this battle with me, that she cared so much about me and my boy. And I don't think the leap to our deep, abiding friendship would've been nearly as quick had she not forgiven me for my idiocy that snowy night and had we not shared deep love for this wise, little, old-soul of a dog. I loved Bunker. Melissa loved him too, which made me love her more.

In the kitchen that night, I told Chris about Bunker's diagnosis. Something in me wanted to stop myself from showing the deep distress I felt. I worried that everything would change if I let the men in the house see my weaknesses. They would see me as someone with crazy problems. To say I was averse to men having a negative opinion of me would be a gross understatement. I was terrified, but trying my best not to show it.

I watched Chris put his hand on his mouth as I spoke, and I hugged him back when he pulled me in saying, "Oh, Jul, I'm so sorry." As if he could hear my thoughts, Chris said, "You doing the surgery then?" Bunker's demise was simply not an option. I smiled, another ally in my corner, and said, "Yep. I'll sell lemonade on the curb and get two more jobs if I have to."

Chris clapped his hands together and smiled. "Let's raise some money," he said, in his indomitable way, his spirit so lively and energetic, his athletic, six-foot frame bouncing, his gestures deep and wide. He rubbed his hands back and forth cooking up a plan. Chris was a man unafraid, undeterred by any potential judgment—and I nearly cried as he stood before me planning what he'd already called *The Bunker Kegger.* "How much do we need?" he asked.

"Four thousand." I squeezed my eyes closed, opened one to peek at Chris's reaction to this gargantuan amount of money.

"Whoa. Okay." I felt engulfed by doubt, ready for the quiet *you're on your own* passivity of the average, defeated, not-my-problem kind of guy. But Chris said, "Well, gotta start somewhere. We'll have a keg, put a bucket next to it with Bunk's picture, ask for donations. And we'll invite everyone. I swear, people will each give you at least twenty bucks." My tears began again. "A hundred people, $20 each, two parties. BOOM! We're all set." I laughed and cried. Chris handed me a dishtowel for my tears and grabbed a pen off the counter. BUNKER KEGGER he wrote on the refrigerator calendar. "Next weekend good?" he said. I nodded and he hugged me again.

I was sitting at the dining room table late that night, looking at my laptop and trying, for the first time, to access this thing people called the Internet. I was trying to sell bootlegged copies of the Halloween Ani DiFranco concert I'd attended at The Paramount Theater. I asked for $10 a tape, and a few people on Ani's fan e-mail list ordered them. Melissa and Chris were already in bed, and Greg came in the front door. We made real, sustained eye contact, the first time since the Glenn fiasco. My stomach sank when our eyes met.

He put his backpack on the futon, sat down, and unlaced his shoes. I didn't say anything. He came to the table, sat down in the chair next to mine, and said, "I heard." I kept my eyes on the laptop, trying to hold back tears. I missed him. I missed his touch, his kiss, his kindness. But, right now, I knew I didn't deserve him. "Chris told me on the phone. Four thousand?" he asked. The tears dripped down my cheeks, and I wanted to explode with apologies, begging Greg to forgive me. I thought of our talks in bed, our efforts to not laugh too loud as we shared stories and had begun falling in love. Why did I have to sabotage it? Why did Bunker have to be so broken?

"I'm so sorry," I muttered. Greg went to the kitchen. I assumed he was not ready for my stupid apology. I put my head in my hands, so incredibly angry at myself. I felt something on the back of my hand. Greg had gone through the kitchen to the TV room to get a box of tissues. He handed it to me and sat back down. I looked at him, wondering if I could ever possibly be worthy of his love.

"I can loan you the money," he said. "I have it. I've been saving money since I was a kid. I can give you the money you need to make Bunker better."

If an earthquake had tumbled me out of my chair and down Queen Anne Hill, I would've been less moved. Greg made pennies as a grad student. He had a small stipend that he lived on. He was as broke as the rest of us, but he still offered me his savings. I shook my head. "Thank you," I said. "That's so generous of you. You're just so amazing and kind. I can't accept it. I can't. But thank you."

He put his hand on mine, as if he wanted to hold it, or say something. Instead he just squeezed gently, stood up, and walked upstairs to his room.

The Bunker Kegger

February 1997

The party was set for that next Saturday night. Greg and Chris picked up the keg and lugged it up the front stairs. Greg and I hadn't talked about Glenn, but he wasn't entirely avoiding me. I assumed he needed more time to think about things, as did I. Will was still calling, but I found myself slightly less engaged by the conversations and often found ways to get off the phone quickly.

Greg and Chris pulled the keg across the living room and Bunker watched with curiosity as they lifted it into a bright-blue bucket and poured ice all around.

"Grocery store?" Melissa said. We drove to the Safeway at the top of the hill and stocked up on chips and salsa, pretzels, and M&Ms. In the checkout line at the store, Melissa said, "I got this. Put that money in the Bunker donation bucket." I protested but she refused my money, and I stood humbled by the generosity of my friends.

I perused the magazines at the checkout stand, not reading a word, just brimming with gratitude, wondering how I had found myself in this wonderful place. Melissa said hello to the cashier and I looked out the tall window at the greenness of this city, contemplating the kindness of the average Northwestern stranger and the sweetness of the fertile air. The wind brushed the tops of the evergreens in the parking lot on top of Queen Anne Hill, and I wanted to know what the wind was telling me. Was it a warning? A sign to be prepared for the coming tragedy? Or was it the same wind in the pine grove in Ohio, the one enveloping me, telling me that despite all the trouble around me, I would be okay?

"You okay?" Melissa asked, as she put the key into the ignition of her rag-top Cabriolet. She'd had the car since high school and we joked about how we always knew she was pulling up to the house because the car sounded like a souped-up lawn mower.

"Yeah," I said quietly. "Actually, I'm good. I'm really good. I'm excited about this party. I think Bunker is too." I fought the flash of frigid dread thinking about Bunker's potential demise. My mind tripped back into the veterinary surgeon's office. I could smell the doctor's cologne mixed with the alcohol used to clean the metal tables. My heart raced, my throat constricted, as I once again considered his words, "... *won't live two years without treatment. One of the worst cases we've ever seen.*"

I wanted to tell Melissa how terrified I was, how desperately I needed Bunker to be okay, how I planned to jump in front of a truck if he died during surgery. Already I'd imagined scenarios of the veterinarian getting distracted, slipping with the scalpel and cutting a major artery, Bunker bleeding out onto the floor, his tongue hanging inert through his teeth. I'd pictured it all and worse. I watched my still-depressed mind develop a sinister plan. Most certainly, if Bunker didn't survive, neither would I.

People arrived at about ten. Friends from all corners of Seattle appeared at our door with cash in hand: graduate students from Greg's lab, office mates from my temp job and Chris's video editing company, Melissa's college friends and co-workers. The bucket at the center of the dining room table began filling and Bunker's happy picture in front of it was soon half hidden with dollar bills.

I stood at the table telling everyone about Bunker's diagnosis. Halfway through the night, I was overcome because we had created a circle of healing. People cared, and they showed it. They held their hands over their mouths as I explained Bunker's debilitating condition. They knelt down in front of him as he leaned against me through much of the party, and they petted his soft head. He watched us all, making eye contact, letting his mouth fall open into a goofy smile, his long red tail feathers swishing back and forth. Bunker leaned into me as I spoke to people. I was his partner, and everyone here loved our connection.

A few hours into the gathering, Chris and I stood in the kitchen and counted the money. We had almost four hundred dollars, and he advised I hide it in my room, just for safekeeping. I slipped it in between my mattress and box spring and noticed that Bunker had retreated to his crate, his eyes bloodshot and sleepy. As if we were connected psychically, I felt a searing pain in my lower back and hip. But I didn't worry that there was something wrong with me.

He couldn't keep his eyes open as I sat down in front of the crate, noting that he was often tired too soon, too mellow and slow for a puppy. "We got you, buddy," I said, easy tears coming again. "We'll fix this." A moment of recognition came and I thought of my father, trying his best to help me, to fix me when I was deeply depressed. I had a glimpse of the desperation he must have felt in the face of my suffering. But I had learned from his determination that even the biggest, scariest problems almost always had a solution.

ON TOUR

FEBRUARY 1997

Will called again, this time to tell me that he was coming to Seattle. His new band was doing a West Coast tour. They were a hard-core punk band and they were playing in a club only a few miles from my house. "I'll be there in one week," he said. I knew that his arrival would bring mixed emotions for both of us. Part of me still wasn't over him. Part of me still loved him because the way things ended left me reeling, without closure. I told him I'd come see his show.

When he called, saying he was in town, my stomach lurched. I wanted to see him, but I was trying hard to remember that he had betrayed me. When he asked me to come to the bar during their 6 p.m. sound check, I reluctantly agreed. But I couldn't imagine going alone. I needed a friend. Melissa was busy, and it would've been more awkward to show up with her than alone.

So I took Bunker with me. I told Will to meet me outside the bar, that I had someone important that I wanted him to meet. I also figured Bunker was a good excuse not to stay long. If Will didn't love my dog, my choice was easy. Would he sink to his knees and pet Bunker? Would he acknowledge him at all?

I walked up the sidewalk with Bunker on a leash and saw Will, his unmistakable silhouette, skinny legs swimming in baggy jeans. He saw me too and started walking. We hugged and the first thing he said was, "You brought your dog?"

"I wanted you two to meet," I said. "Bunker, this is Will. Will, this is Bunker."

"Well, he can't come into the venue," Will said, and right then I knew.

"I know," I said. "I can't stay. I just wanted to say hi."

"You all good? You okay?" Will asked. In his words I heard questions I wasn't willing to address.

"Yep," I said. "I'm doing great. I love Seattle. So much more than New York."

"Well, I don't know about that," Will said.

"Well, it was good to see you. Have a great show tonight." And with that, Bunker and I turned around and walked away. This wasn't the last time I would see Will, but it was the first time I knew we weren't right together. It was the first time I knew it was best for me to move on.

LOSING GREG

FEBRUARY 1997

Greg asked if we could talk. I knew the conversation about my betrayal was inevitable, but I didn't know Greg well enough yet to know how it would go. I had been dreading it for weeks, imagining him shaming me, calling me a whore. When Melissa and Chris were gone and Greg invited me to join him in the living room for a talk, I lingered in the kitchen, cursing under my breath.

He sat on the futon upon which we'd shared our first kiss. I remembered the sweet words he'd said, *"Man, I've been waiting a long time to do that."* I sat on the edge of the wicker chair across from him. The chair flipped up and wobbled, detached from its base, forcing me to scoot back, sit deeply in the seat, commit to this conversation.

"I want to talk about what happened," Greg said, clasping his hands.

"Yeah," I said. He was silent and I looked down, studied the floor. "I'm an asshole."

"Well, what you did was something an asshole does, yes," he smirked a bit, and I could sense that enough time had passed, and he wasn't as hurt as he was confused. He wanted to know if he'd done something wrong, if I didn't like him the way he thought I did. He looked so vulnerable. Who was this man? Who was I in relation to this sweet, gentle man?

In the few months we'd lived together, I'd come to understand that deep down, Greg was good. He was thoughtful, brilliant, and funny. He was a child of intellectuals. He was a man with kind and gentle eyes, bluer than any Caribbean shallows, and he sat across from me, terribly sad. I had hurt him deeply, he said, and he told me that when he went home for his Christmas break, he sat in his mom's house and moped. "Everyone asked me if I was okay, but I just brushed them off."

"Did you say anything about me?" I asked.

"No," he said. Hadn't he wanted to tell his mom that he'd tried dating his housemate? That she seemed lovely before she shredded his heart to bits?

"I just feel like," I said, uncertain, averting my eyes, "like I need to be single right now."

"Really?" he said, his voice sharp, riddled with surprise. "But what about all that stuff we talked about, what we were doing, I mean ..." his voice trailed off. He swept his hand through his hair and sighed deeply.

"I don't know," I said. "Maybe I don't. I'm just really confused. Bunker has me so worried, and the first surgery is next week, and I just can't focus."

He nodded, "Yeah, I'll bet. Poor Bunk," he said.

We were silent a few moments. I didn't know what I wanted. I had never been faced with this: a man who seemed so good and kind, who was straightforward and not dishonest or jealous. Still, all I wanted was to give every ounce of myself to Bunker. I didn't want a boyfriend. Yet, a very strong candidate for a good, healthy relationship had presented himself. A truck rumbled up the hill and rattled the one-paned living room windows. We both looked toward the street, then Greg said, "I want us to try to be together. I think we'd be great."

In my long history of serial relationships, no one had ever put it so simply, so directly. But I couldn't hear it. I only thought of Bunker, and of his failing body. Ever since the diagnosis, my nerves had been jangled, my focus terrible. It was no different sitting across from this good man.

"Did you hear me?" he asked, quietly, pleadingly.

"Yes," I said. "But I just can't."

He closed his eyes and took a long, deep breath.

"I just need to be alone right now. I can't be in a relationship." The pain in his eyes made me look away. What was I doing? What the hell was I doing? Resolve settled in me. This was the first time I'd tried choosing myself over a relationship, and the feeling was empowering.

Then he said, quietly, "Well, then I need to move out." A beat later he said, "I can't be here in this house with you if we aren't going to give it a shot. It would just be torture for me. I'm sorry."

My family, the new one we had all created, that had cradled and helped me through the beginning of Bunker's health crisis, was falling apart thanks to my thoughtless actions. I fought off tears, and said, "But I don't want you to go." The intensity of feeling behind those words weren't conveyed in how I said them. I wanted to beg him. *Please, please, please. Don't leave yet.*

"Don't," I blurted without thinking. "Don't move out yet."

"But I'm going to have to."

"Please don't," I said. "Please. Just wait a while. Until after Bunker's surgery."

"It'll just be too hard to stay," he said. "I'm sorry." I pictured him loading his meager belongings into his crappy little car and driving to a sad new studio. No. That just wouldn't do.

"Please?" I asked. "Wait a while before you make a decision."

He looked at Bunker who was asleep and dreaming on the floor between us. Greg didn't respond. He just stood up and slowly went up the stairs to his room.

He Dies, I Die

February 1997

The sun shone ominously on the morning of Bunker's surgery. Of course, rain would've felt like a bad sign too. I woke up and slid down to the floor next to Bunk. He yawned, the great crevasse of his toothy mouth and blindingly white teeth a reminder that he was an animal, not a magical, mythical cure-all. He stretched his back legs as if they were perfectly healthy. He lay down next to me, his body fully aligned with mine. Then he rolled on his back. I petted his hip, the left one, which would be the first operated on today. The right hip would be opened up in four weeks.

Today, he was to skip breakfast and arrive at the clinic before eight. At exactly nine o'clock, the hair on his left hip would be shaved off from his spine all the way down to his ankle. The skin would be sliced open in two eight-inch incisions and his pelvic bone would be sawed apart in three places. They would then rotate his bone and secure it with plates and screws so that the hip cradled his femur at the proper angle. He'd just turned eight months old. With this surgery, he had some chance of normal development. Without it: the unspeakable.

The Bunker Kegger had raised five hundred dollars. I'd saved five hundred from my job, and my parents sent me a check for a thousand dollars. My mom included a piece of paper with a repayment plan, $200 a month for five months. The money was in my account, the checkbook next to my purse.

I closed my eyes and inhaled the nape of Bunker's neck, not wanting to exhale and let this day begin. I held my breath in an effort to stop the seconds from peeling on, from the anesthetic taking him out of this world for even a moment, for me not being with him as he shook with fright as the well-meaning veterinary technician took him away from me. I wondered if it would be okay for me to write a note and attach it to his collar: *This is not just any dark-red golden. This is no ordinary family dog. This is my lifeline to this world, and though you may not understand or may think I am overstating, please believe that he is the one reason I am still here. Please care for him like he was your own baby, just eight months old, the love of your life, the reason for your life. Please care for him like your life depends on it. If he is okay and well soon, I will be forever and eternally grateful.*

The clock read seven-thirty. I took him out the front door so he could pee in the grass. I sat on the front stoop thinking that this was the last time for a while that my boy would be able to descend the stairs himself. I would have to carry him, all fifty plus pounds of him, up and down the steps for the next several weeks. His tail swirled as he sniffed the weeds in the sidewalk, checking every few minutes to make sure I was still sitting on the stoop, watching him. "Good boy," I said, smiling. "You're the best boy."

I noticed that the mailbox was full from yesterday. We were all still getting the hang of this adult life, and sometimes we didn't pick up the mail for days. I stood up and emptied the box; junk mail flapping down to the porch floor, bills and letters entangled in mangled newsprint. I sat down with the mail on my lap and sorted the letters—bills for the house, a letter for Melissa from Ohio, credit card solicitations.

At the bottom of the pile sat a blue envelope hand-addressed to me in the unmistakable slanty jag of Clay's hand. I stared at the card for a moment, then opened it gently. Bunker loped up the porch stairs and lay down next to me with a thud. The card had a cartoon of a teddy bear in bed with a blue ice bag on its head. Clay wrote, "Julie, Sorry to hear about Bunker. I am sure he will be fine. He is in our prayers. Here's a check for the surgery fund."

I closed the card slowly, looked at the front cover, then opened it up again. I read his note over and over. It made me so happy that he had done this, but also oddly angry. Then I remembered what all of the therapists had said about how his abuse had hurt me, forever altered me, even changed my brain chemistry. And I decided that very moment to forgive myself for believing Clay.

We were both hurting as kids, and his way of coping with his pain was to turn to anger, to turn it toward me. My way of coping was to turn to sorrow and turn against myself. I saw it so clearly at that moment, holding his get-well card for Bunker. I held the paper and forgave the little girl who just wanted her big brother to love and protect her. I told her that it was okay to want his love, and that I was sorry that she didn't get it.

Then something amazing happened. Once I forgave myself, I felt as if I could forgive my brother. I would never forget, but I could forgive. I could forgive Will for not returning my love when I was in New York. I could forgive my father for his absences, my mother for her emotional unavailability. What if, I thought, I can even forgive myself for sleeping with Glenn and for being a bad friend? What if I could forgive myself for being an ungrateful daughter? What if I just decided that all of those mistakes were teachings? Maybe all of those choices I'd made were so that I could learn that what I wanted wasn't drama and sorrow, just love: love in the way Bunker gave love. Unconditional. No expectations. No strings. Just love, because what is more beautiful than that?

I held Clay's one hundred dollar check in my hand, fingering his signature and wondering whether my mom had suggested that he send me money or he had decided to do it himself. Either way, I decided, this was fine. Everything was okay. I was going to think positively all day. I was going to hold my thoughts in a bright, happy, Bunker place. And with that energy, Bunker would pull through just fine.

I stood up, went inside, got dressed, and clipped the leash on Bunker's collar. He hopped a little, probably thinking that this would be our usual walk to the park. I helped him into the car, then left Queen Anne, drove down through Fremont and into Wallingford. The sun blared, and I didn't celebrate. I appreciated the sun as much as the rain: there was goodness in both.

I squinted and Bunker walked warily through the surgery center's glass doors. After I signed the papers and wrote the check, a vet technician said he could come with her. I gave her his leash. The words *dear god, dear god, dear god* looped in my mind, a panicked appeal that my boy would survive this day. I pressed down thoughts of blood-soaked floors, the saw slipping, an unfortunate twitch with scalpel in hand. I knelt next to Bunker, who was pulling on the leash, trying to get back to me and away from the funny-smelling lady wearing scrubs with rainbow-colored paw prints.

"It'll be okay, buddy," I whispered. "Be strong. You'll be okay. I'll see you tomorrow. You'll have one night here and I'll be back the second they call me." Reassuring him calmed me and I put my cheek next to his and whispered, "I love you."

I tried to wipe away my tears. I decided that I looked like an idiot in front of this receptionist and another man and woman sitting in the waiting room. My mind conjured a room full of people scowling and saying, *No one likes you. That dog's the only one who will ever love you because he's stupid and doesn't know better.* I nodded and turned away, walked outside with my hand on my mouth. I told myself to stop. *Be positive. Think positive.*

I started back to the house but panic rose mere blocks from the clinic. *If he dies, I die. If he dies, I die.* I couldn't stop the thoughts, and I began hyperventilating. "Oh, my god," I said, again and again. I parked on Taylor Avenue, raced up the front stairs, and climbed into bed. I had an hour to get to work, but I couldn't even manage to look at the clock. My thoughts raced and I followed. I tried to take a breath but choked with the thought of Bunker in that cold, scary operating room without me.

I managed to pull myself together enough to get to the office, sit down at the reception desk, organize the inter-office mail, and make a pot of coffee. I was buzzing, and the dark coolness of the office lobby, the predictable routine of this job, helped distract me. The office was on the twentieth floor with black-tinted windows. We joked about how the building's architect must've been from California because no building in Seattle needed help filtering the sun.

By two o'clock, the wait to hear from the vet made me feel as if I had a tin can between my ears. I felt light and full of air; as if I might try to take a breath and *poof*, drift off through the hole in the ozone and out into space. Thoughts going: *Is Bunker still alive at this very second? Is he awake? Is he aware of anything? Is he in pain? Did something go terribly wrong?*

"Olson and Smithfield," I said. "How may I direct your call?" Each call could've been the veterinarian with terrible news, or the vet receptionist calling to tell me my check had bounced.

"Julie?" A voice said. I couldn't place who it was.

"Uh, yes," I said. "This is Julie. How can I help you?"

"It's your brother," the voice said. I would never have guessed that the voice on the phone belonged to Clay. "Mom told me today was the big day," he said. "I just wanted to tell you I am thinking about you and I know Bunker will pull through just fine." My mouth opened to speak, but nothing came. I couldn't shake the fact that I had a brother, and that I did not know his voice. It rang strangely tinny, as if the vocal chamber was sure of the words, but the mouth wasn't convinced about how they should emerge. "You there? Hello?" he asked. I was staring at the empty lobby of this law firm. It was noon, usually the time most attorneys, paralegals, and secretaries were heading to lunch, walking from the break room to their desks clutching microwaved plates. But there was no one around. Not a soul.

This law office could've been my father's law office, where he sat so many days working while Clay and I fought in our suburban home. It was as if I had switched alliances, no longer loyal to my family. I was testing out my own loyalty to the law, to my own justice, to my new family. All of this passed through my mind, then I wondered if I was dreaming when I heard myself say, "Thanks ... Thanks for calling."

"No problem," he said. "Good luck. He'll be okay." It sounded as if he was already moving on to the next task. I don't remember the rest of the call, or exactly how it ended, except that I felt both moved and uncomfortable. Did he hang up and scoff that I was so stupidly attached to a stupid dog? Did he immediately tell my mom that he'd called me—just like she asked? Why did I care? Good heavens, why did I care so goddamned much about what Clay thought of me? And then I remembered again to try to forgive the little girl who wanted her brother to love her. It was okay. He'd called and that was nice.

I found myself mentioning to anyone who stopped by the reception desk that I'd just gotten off the phone with my brother. When people would ask how I was, I'd say, "Good. My brother just called." Even three hours later, I was still telling people, "I talked to my brother today," just to see how that sounded.

At the front desk I bent open paper clips into long spears, lining them up like knives on notebook paper, one centimeter apart. The phone rang all afternoon, but no veterinarian. A discomfort in my chest left me patting my sternum with my fist. It felt like a giant man was sitting on my heart. I tried to take a deep breath. Couldn't.

Bunker, I whispered. I felt him slipping away. I imagined him dead on a metal gurney, the vet standing with Bunker's head in his hands. Failed. Mistaken. I would die. I stood up, walked to the window forty stories high, and realized with face-flushing terror: It was right here. The depression. The awful dread. It was right here all along. Maybe it had never left. Maybe I would never be rid of it. It was just waiting until Bunker left and then it would attack again.

That moment, as I imagined Bunker being gone, I thought, *I don't care if I die.* I walked to the window, thirty-eight floors up, and put my hands on the glass, so grateful it didn't open. I shivered. My parents were right: Seattle *was* cold. "Bunker," I whispered, tapping an outstretched paper clip on the window, then stepping back and bending it back to its original state. "Please be okay."

When the veterinarian finally called, I knew it before I picked up the receiver. I knew they had news of my boy. I was standing at the fax machine when the phone rang. I dropped the papers and sprinted to the desk, losing one shoe in the rush.

"Hello?" I said, and in that moment I heard a girl's voice saying *This is blah blah from Seattle Animal Surgical Center* and time pulled down, slowed, nearly stopped, and I didn't breathe. In those few seconds as I waited for their news, I planned to stand in front of their clinic, then step in front of an oncoming truck if they'd killed him. I had my quick death planned, and the turn in my gut was sour and awful and I was back on my New York apartment's floorboards.

"We wanted to let you know," she said, slowly, agonizingly, "that Bunker is resting now. He's doing fine and the surgery was successful." All the screeching stopped. It was like someone yelled, *Cut!* The drama was over. I shamed myself, hated that I'd made such a dramatic, stupid, histrionic, and sinister plan. The pattern was familiar. After the rush of adrenaline, the fallout. The blame. *What a stupid idiot. What a dumb little sister.*

"Okay. Thank you," I said. *You're so dumb. You're an idiot.* My depression yelled at me from the back of my mind, angry that it had been defeated. "Thank you so much. Thank you. You have no idea how relieved I am. How happy I am, I mean."

"You can come pick him up after 9 a.m. tomorrow," she said. "He'll be ready to go, and please re-read the discharge instructions so you're prepared to get him into the car and then from the car to your house."

"Okay," I said. "I'm ready for him. Everything's all set up." And with that, the awful voice in my head popped like a child's balloon.

Bunker needed me. I was *needed*. My beloved dog, my spirit twin, the one who saved me, the one I had just saved. I had a job to do. I was going to nurse my boy back to health. I had memorized those discharge instructions. I had prepared my bedroom and Bunker's crate, as if I were expecting a brand-new baby. I'd lined the floor of his crate with colorful blankets and cushions, opened the top of the crate so he could stick his head out and stretch if he needed to. I put the crate next to the opened window and pushed my bed next to it, so that, just like when he was a puppy in that crate, I could sleep with one hand on his shoulder. I bought him a squeaky lambskin toy and propped it in the corner.

I still had a hard time taking care of myself, but having something else to take care of helped me. I was useful now. I could recognize pain in Bunker's face, and his eyes, his other-worldly, deep, soulful eyes full of all the pain and laughter and hope of all our combined longing, helped me see that I was hurting inside too. It helped me forgive myself, because I knew Bunker wouldn't want me to hurt. When I was happy, he was thrilled. I wanted his happiness, and through it I found my own. As I watched the clock tick toward the end of my workday and the beginning of my race to pick up Bunker, I thought about how his outer scars were like my inner scars. I would recognize them, tend to them, help them slowly heal, and do my best to care for both of us, with every ounce of my being.

Reunited

February 1997

"He's going to want to run," the nurse said. I sat in an examination room waiting for Bunker to enter. "But he can't. For four weeks he needs to be kept fairly still. The first week, I want him contained in his crate every minute—only carry him outside to do his business. The second week, he can walk, but only inside and no hardwood floors, no stairs. Only carpets. The third week, he can go outside on a leash with you still carrying him up and down stairs. Still no hardwoods. For a whole month."

She continued speaking when the door clicked open. Bunker. His back left leg hairless and pink. Two enormous incision scars, one seven inches long, the other about five inches, with twenty-six Frankensteinian staples lining the incisions. The shock of it for one split second, and then his eyes. Our eyes. They met and he was still there, we were still there together. Nothing had taken him, his spirit, his healing, and he pulled toward me, whining, whimpering, and I sank down and let him come to me. The nurse held his leash tight. He walked to me, his back legs moving with a barely perceptible limp. "See, he thinks he's fine. He doesn't know the extent of the trauma in there. So it's your job to force him to take it easy, to take care of himself so he can heal properly."

"Yes, of course. You're okay, buddy," I said. "You'll be okay." He lay down on the cool floor, healthy hip down, and he licked my neck, my ears, whimpering, howling a little. My whole body tingled. He wasn't even a year old yet, and this. He'd been through *this*. The incisions were long and curved, and the staples looked so much like medieval torture, they gave me prickly chills. I closed my eyes and inhaled him, felt him again, his softness, his calm. "Oh, my angel," I said.

Too much pain too early in life could change this beautiful animal forever. But too much pain followed by a loving caregiver, a loving parent? That can end up just fine. This, I knew. I turned to my puppy, letting myself fall into our love, our relationship, our miracle.

"You'll be running again soon," I whispered. "We'll be running together." He rested his muzzle on my neck, a deep, deep sigh from him. He was exhausted, but he was home. We, together, no matter where we landed, we were home.

I drove back to the house from the veterinary hospital with one hand reaching back to hold Bunker's leg. He lay in the back seat, still a little drugged and completely worn out. When we pulled up to the house, I parked, opened the front door then went back to the car to get him. He tried to stand but couldn't. "Shhh, shhh," I said. "I got you, buddy." I pushed my arms under his body and carried him out of the car like he was as light as a down pillow. My strength and steadiness were unwavering. I walked up each step, no wobbling, no straining, just my voice in his soft ear. "You're okay," I whispered, over and over. I brought him into my bedroom and bent over the opened top of the metal crate. "Here we go, bud," I said. "We're going to hang out here for a while." His tail wagged slightly at the sound of my voice. I lowered him slowly, carefully, feeling no muscle strain, no stress to my body. Every muscle was dedicated to the healing of his body now, and that left me feeling stronger than ever, devoid of all complaint.

"There you go," I said, whispering. The tone I had was my mother's. I heard her voice soothing me as a child. I felt her calloused hand on my neck, pulling my hair away from my face. "It's okay to cry," I said to my dog, and I was my father. I was my wonderful dad on the lake asking me to tell him everything. "It's okay for you to whimper. It hurts. You have every right to howl about that."

I sat in the chair next to Bunker's crate, whispering to him as he fell asleep. I felt as if I could sit there at his bedside watching and caring for him for months, years, as long as it took. If he had to be stuck in his crate, isolated from the world, I would sit with him. I would not let him suffer alone.

What surprised me after several minutes of holding vigil crateside was that I was smiling. I absolutely knew that Bunker would heal and run again. Outside, cars drove by, wind blew the enormous pine in the front yard, birds swooped overhead, and I sat silent in prayerful meditation next to my boy, relieved and hopeful because he was still alive, and we were together again.

The nurse was right. Bunker wanted to run before he could walk. The first day home, he whimpered to leave the crate. I opened the door and he stood up, holding his back leg up off the ground, clearly in pain. I squatted in front of the open crate door and talked to him. "Listen, buddy. You need to go slow. Take it easy. I will carry you outside to pee and sniff, but no walking. Got it?" He looked at me blankly, and I called him out of the crate. He limped out and did not resist when I put one arm under his chest and another under his stomach and lifted him off the ground. I had already opened the front door. I slowly descended the stairs, Bunker patiently waited to be put down.

He peed, hobbled a few steps, and then looked at me as if to say he was ready to go back to bed now. I carried him inside and settled him gently in his crate, gave him his painkillers wrapped in a slice of deli ham. He swallowed without chewing, lay down, and his eyes immediately drooped with fatigue. He would open them periodically as if to make sure I was still there, and to ask, "You okay? You doing okay?"

"I'm good, buddy," I said, out loud. "And you're going to be great in no time, my brave little warrior."

All Out or All In

March 1997

One cloudy afternoon, three weeks after the first surgery, Greg asked me if I could come to the living room. Melissa and Chris were gone when he sat down and said, "I need to know what we're doing."

"What?" I asked, knowing exactly what he meant but wanting only to continue walking, to take Bunker outside for some fresh air. Bunker was recovering beautifully, could walk up the street now. I added half a block a day to our walk. He was up to seven blocks. He just needed help on stairs and had to follow the path of rugs from the bedroom to the kitchen and back. The next surgery would be in about three weeks, and I felt confident I could nurse him back to full health. I imagined that maybe in a few months we'd be walking at Marymoor together, him frolicking pain-free, me behind him, soaking up his joy.

"Now that the surgery's over, I need to know if I should start looking for another place, move out," Greg said. It was clear that he had struggled for days to muster the courage to talk to me. I could feel the heavy words clunking on the ground at my feet.

I sat down across from him with reluctance. "I don't know," I said. I truly didn't.

"I need to know," he said, and I registered a tiny twinge of anger in his voice.

"I don't know," I said. "I'm just confused. I'm really confused. I..."

He squeezed his eyes closed, then looked at his feet, his elbows on his knees, his hands wringing around each other. "That tells me something," he said, his voice distant and flat.

"No, it's not that," I stuttered. "I just don't think I can be in a relationship right now."

"I get it," he said, his jawbone pulsing.

I didn't know what to say. I desperately longed to go outside and sprint up the hill until I was breathless, until my lungs burned for mercy. Then, I thought, in pain, in physical distress, I might see more clearly. "Okay," I said. I stood up and called Bunker. He came to me quietly, his tail wagging. I hooked on the leash and held open the door, sneaking one last look at Greg a moment before walking out. He still had his elbows on his knees, his head dropped in defeat.

Bunker walked outside with me and stopped on the front porch. I longed to run to the farthest, darkest edges of Seattle. I imagined running to a ferryboat and somehow hoofing it into the Olympic Mountains, where I could collapse in the wettest rainforest I could find. I imagined lying there waiting for the lichen to grow on me, for the enormous slugs to trudge across my chest, into my ears.

"Come on, Bunk," I said. I picked him up and walked down the stairs. My vision blurred from tears. Bunker took two slow, trudging steps and then began walking, ever the willing partner despite his pain and broken bones. *I am so stupid,* I thought. The thoughts kept coming, an echo chamber of all I'd done wrong. But I could see the thoughts like black clouds, and they went away just as quickly as they came. I forgave myself for them. And I stopped on the sidewalk just a few houses up from ours, sat down next to Bunker, and held his neck against my face. "I'm sorry," I whispered, stroking his neck. I took a deep breath of him, his alive, earthy scent. "I'm so sorry, my sweetest friend," I whispered into his neck.

Bunker wagged his tail and took a step, as if the shift in my behavior was satisfactory, so I stood up and began walking too. Slowly, steadily, we walked away from the house. Bunker looked up at me, opened his mouth into a smile, and we crossed the street together.

One block in, I was making the case for not having another boyfriend, for not needing another heartbreak in my still semi-fragile state. Then I thought about how this romance had been going so differently, that I was pushing this man and his kindness away. I thought of my therapist in Ohio explaining that it made sense that relationships left me insecure and heartbroken, because that was what I brought to them. Feeling terrible, she told me, felt comfortable. "So you seek out that feeling in your romances," she explained. "I know it seems too simple, but consider it."

After walking one block, I was trying to wrap my head around what it might be like to embark upon a different kind of relationship. Greg had offered me part of his childhood savings to heal my dog. He'd made me laugh with all of my body. He was brilliant and driven, but also kind. His middle-of-the-night touch felt like a homecoming. But I still didn't feel like I needed him.

After two blocks, I panicked. Maybe this is what healthy love was supposed to feel like. Maybe I wasn't supposed to need him. Maybe I was supposed to love to be with him, but also love to be without him. The concept struck me as totally unromantic, not passionate enough. The fire in all of my love affairs had been their desperation.

After three blocks, I wondered if maybe that's why they burned out.

Four blocks in, I decided to just consider Greg. All the things about him. His blue eyes. His soft hands. His generosity. His humor. His wanting *me*, not the coifed, make-up wearing me, but the me who padded around in pajama pants and a ripped T-shirt on a hungover Sunday morning.

Five blocks in, I stopped. I closed my eyes and I thought of the last time he climbed into my bed at two in the morning, before Glenn. His right hand was the first thing to press on my mattress, the weight of him making me fall toward him, his left hand on my neck, his lips on mine, my pulling the covers over him, wrapping his arms all the way around me like he was a soldier just back from war. Once I felt like I might cry surprising, out-of-nowhere tears of joy at his mere arrival.

Six blocks in, I stopped.

Bunker stopped with me, looking up to watch for my next turn. At each street corner, he stopped and looked up at me. I'd trained him to do that. When we stopped at the corner of Nob Hill and Newton Street, he watched me for an indication of where to go. To the field? Home? Usually he pulled toward the field. But today he didn't. Today he sat calmly, watching my eyes. When I nodded and looked down the road back toward home, he took the first steps, and I followed.

I carried him back up the steps to the house. He licked my wrists as I picked him up, an act of submission and thanks. I placed him gingerly on the front porch and opened the door, hoping to see Greg on the futon still, waiting for me to come back.

The house sounded empty, minus Bunker walking along the carpet trail toward his water bowl. How I adored the sound of him messily lapping up water, half of it landing on his snout, his forehead, and the floor. When he finished, there was silence, and I stood by the closed front door holding the leash, listening. I sprinted up the stairs and saw Greg's door was closed. *Please be there. Please be there. Please be there.*

I knocked twice, nothing. Two more times, nothing. I twisted the doorknob and pushed open the door and saw his feet crossed at the foot of his bed. He was lying there, looking at nothing, the sorrow around him nearly visible. I sat down on the edge of his mattress and extended my hand toward him. He stayed perfectly still, staring at his slanted ceiling. I heard Bunker downstairs, thudding to my bedroom floor, groaning, tired after our walk.

"I just," I stumbled. "I changed my mind." Greg tried to not show any emotion, but the tiniest smile crept to his face. I knew he was angry, and he didn't want to smile, and I loved that he couldn't help it.

"You're a little bit of an asshole," he said. "Again."

"I know. I know. I am. I'm learning. You have to understand," I began. "I am not used to a kind man. I'm not used to a nice guy who actually wants to be with me. I don't know. How do I explain this? You're not a jerk. You're a nice person. You're kind and sensitive. That's new to me. But I need someone who will stick through the shit with me," I said. The words felt like tumbling bricks out of me. "Because I am warning you now, I bring a lot of shit. I carry it inside me for some reason, and you never know when I'm going to open and it's going to be rancid and awful and you're going to wonder why the hell you ever chose me."

"Maybe," he said. "Unlikely, though."

His palpable relief at my return left me squirmy and uncomfortable. Why would he want to be with me so much? I needed to tell him what he was getting himself into, so I started talking. "I was fucked up as a kid. Not like terrible fucked up, but I think I got a really warped self-image. And I have been in some bad relationships, and I'm not a hundred percent well."

I wanted to say the words *I have depression.* The weight of those words sat under all my chatter, and the more I spoke, the closer they floated to the top. "Once, I tried to jump out of my dad's car when he was driving down the freeway. And once I wanted my mom to think I was going to stab myself with a knife. I lost my shit in Manhattan. I mean, really. And the only reason I survived last summer was because I got Bunker. I'm unhealthily attached to him, because I was diagnosed..." I could hear my heart beating in my ears. I didn't know if I was telling Greg these things so that he would not want to be with me, or so that we could start out with one hundred percent truth between us. "Ugh," I stopped, coughed, choking a little bit on spit that had flicked itself to the back of my throat just as I tried to eek out the words, "with clinical depression. And I have to take medication so that I won't want to go jump off a bridge for no apparent reason. And I'm trying to get down to the bottom of why I'm like this, why all this happens, and I really am doing so much better, and I'm so happy here in Seattle. I love it here." I was crying now. "And you're so amazing. You're like a light coming to me just when I need it, just when I can't accept it, but I'm just going to try accepting it anyway. If you'll still have me. You are so kind and sweet and funny. And I think I could actually, totally fall in love with you. You're like ..." His face twitched, as if he was trying to determine if he should laugh or run. "Oh, my god, I can't believe I just said that. You must think I'm insane. I'm sorry. It's just that I don't feel that nagging crazy love feeling with you. I feel this kind of sweet, calm love feeling with you and I think I need to maybe follow that ... Oh, god. Don't take that the wrong way. I just feel like maybe this is what a healthy relationship is supposed to feel ..."

I would've kept talking, but he stopped me the only way he knew how, with his lips on mine. He pulled me over to him more forcefully than he ever had, and we were together again, our bodies aligned on his mattress and box spring on the floor, and I pictured something like a double helix swirling up from us, DNA lined with daisies and sunshine and tall grasses and butterflies. Good god, it was beautiful.

We had our first official date a few days later at a French restaurant inside Pike Place Market. Greg suggested that we just try to start over. "Clean slate," he said. After I knew I had a second chance with this man, I vowed never to make the same mistake again. I walked up First Avenue and spotted him standing on the corner of Pike Street clutching a bouquet of tulips. "To new beginnings," he said, handing them to me.

"To new beginnings," I said, taking his hand.

That night I wrote in a new journal that I'd had sitting on my nightstand for weeks. "This is my new journal. We'll see how long this lasts. But I want to write this down because I think I have met the man I want to marry. I want to record this so our kids can see this. But it's odd, because it's a very calm feeling, this."

Second Hip

April 1997

Almost a month later, the night before Bunker's second surgery, Greg slept in my room all through the night. Usually he slipped back to his room around one in the morning, but we fell asleep, and I needed his comfort.

"I think I left my door open last night," Greg whispered in the hallway. "The jig might be up." Melissa didn't say anything, but the way she said good morning told me she knew everything.

"Cat's out of the bag," I said.

"First things first," he said, petting Bunker. "You're top priority today, bud." I sat fighting the urge to think catastrophically, trying to remember the positive thoughts that had calmed me during the first surgery.

Greg drove my truck, and I sat in the back with Bunker on the way to the surgeon's office. Bunker pulled on the leash away from the hospital doors as we approached the building.

"He's no dummy," Greg said.

"Can you give us a minute?" I asked, needing to be alone with my boy.

"Sure. I'll wait inside." Greg seemed unperturbed by my request. He understood that my connection to Bunker was like that of two soul mates, and he didn't try to change it. He didn't feel jealous of my devotion to my dog. On the contrary, he would watch and admire us. He would comment to his friends and family that I was the most incredible dog-whisperer he'd ever seen. He'd say that I could anticipate my dog's needs in a remarkable way, and he'd never met a better dog than Bunker.

I sat on the ground in the parking lot with Bunker, put both my hands on his shoulders and tried to explain. The hair on his left hip was about half an inch long, soft and downy like a baby's. "Remember that awful, confusing thing that happened?" I said, and he sat down in front of me. I wrapped my legs around him. "That's going to happen again, okay?" I said. "It's going to be awful one more time, okay? And then I'll help you, and Greg and Melissa and Chris will help you. And you'll be better, Bunk. You'll be so much better. We can go to Marymoor and *run*. Can you imagine? How wonderful that will be?" He heard the joy in my voice and his tail wagged. A car pulled into the parking lot and a woman noticed me sitting communing with my dog. She smiled at us as she walked past. Oh, how I loved Seattle people.

"You'll be okay," I said. "You can do this." He stood up. "You ready?" I started walking and he hesitated again, then reluctantly walked into the clinic, his tail tucked tight between his legs, his head down. When the receptionist saw him, she remembered him. "Bunker!" she said. "You're back! Oh, we love Bunker!" She turned to me and said, "We all just fell in love with this guy last time he was here. What a great, great dog. Hi, buddy!" Bunker still had his tail tucked between his legs, but it wagged ever so slightly and he whimpered a loud, long half-howl, half-cry.

I put my mouth next to his ear and whispered, "You'll be okay." The receptionist took his leash and walked him back through the swinging door. "What a great boy you are," she said. "We're so happy to see you doing so well. Look, guys! Bunker!" I heard her say.

Greg looked at me and smiled. I couldn't smile back yet. I couldn't really focus on anything. My boy was gone again, and I had to wait one more excruciating day to see if he would be okay. The receptionist came back, beaming and laughing as if she'd just stolen a dose of antidepressants from me. I tried to keep my composure as she explained the procedures to me a second time, reminding me that I would get a phone call around four or five o'clock with news about how the surgery went and that I could pick him up in the morning.

I thanked her, saying a silent prayer, trying to repeat everything I did after I dropped him off for the first surgery. Positive thoughts. Patience. Good things. Greg took my hand as we walked back to the car and I felt shaky. Ominous. I tried to shake it off, buckled myself into the passenger seat, and Greg started driving.

The farther we drove, the worse the ominous feeling became. I realized with a panic that Greg hadn't come with me to drop Bunker off for the first surgery. I had done that alone. I had taken him to the clinic myself, comforted him alone, driven to work alone, and everything had turned out okay. Why had I agreed to let Greg take us to the second surgery? My superstition about this was so intense and real that I burst into terrible sobs, unable to speak, my head in my hands, my breath jagged. I was so heavy with regret that I could hardly breathe. I cried hard. I had never cried like this in front of anyone except my parents and therapists. This was the kind of crying I did in the shower in New York when I feared for my sanity. I couldn't control it. And I couldn't look at Greg. I was terribly embarrassed and convinced that something awful would happen because I'd let this man come with me and I shouldn't have. This was something sacred between Bunker and me. Not Bunker, me, and Greg.

I didn't notice until I began to stop sobbing that Greg had pulled the car over to the side of the road. We were on a busy two-lane highway, but he found a spot to safely pull to the side and turn off the engine.

"He'll be okay," Greg said. "Did you see the way those people greeted him? They're going to take such great care of him."

I nodded, my face still in my hands. I couldn't tell Greg that something had busted open in me—that letting him come with me to drop my beloved off for his second awful, terrible, traumatizing surgery felt too intimate. I wasn't ready to let anyone in like that. I wasn't ready to trust that any man could handle this situation and not turn and run because his new girlfriend was a crazy dog freak. I imagined all the awful things he could say or do—tell me I was nuts, sit silently waiting for me to stop, then not know what to say and leave me apologetic and awkward and deep-down regretting ever letting him see me in such a vulnerable state.

I cradled my face as if there were a hideous disfigurement under my hands, and I couldn't let Greg see. I didn't want to let any light in. I didn't want to look up and see his face. I didn't know what I would find, and I felt such comfort in the darkness with my eyes closed, my face cradled in my palms. This place was too familiar, too real, too inviting. He wasn't speaking, and I didn't dare say anything. I just tried to calm my breathing and keep my face covered. My hands grew hot, my face sweaty. Five minutes passed, then more. I wondered what on earth was going on. Was Greg sleeping? Was he staring at me like I was a zoo animal? Was he at a loss for words?

I finally pulled my hands away from my face and slowly opened my eyes. The cool air on my cheeks and forehead nearly made me shiver. I looked straight ahead—the cars flying past us on our left, the windshield a little bit foggy from my heavy breathing. I turned my head slightly, not sure what I might see.

What I did see was Greg: calm, clear, loving. He tilted his head a little, searched me with his eyes and said three of the most beautiful words I've ever heard, "I'm still here." I knew right then that no matter what, I would never, ever lose this man again.

MARYMOOR

MAY 1997

Bunker made it through his second surgery. He trusted that I would carry him down the stairs for several weeks. He seemed to understand that our walks would stop for a while, but return eventually. He appeared content, as if he knew he'd been saved and would endure the painful recovery so he could soon commence his work on this with me and all who loved him. He would sit in his lidless crate, his chin on my bedroom's opened windowsill, his nose poking out the window. I watched him for hours because he emanated contentedness simply watching a bird alight on a branch on the pine tree. His nose would twitch and he'd sniff furiously when another dog walked by. When the roommates came home, they would come straight to my room, greet Bunker with a howl and a pat, and he would return the howl with his chin high. I marveled at him, because even with his hip shaved naked, dozens of metal staples jutting out at the mark of the two large incisions, he still radiated peacefulness. Even in his confinement, Bunker went from contemplation to tail-wagging glee at the mere scent of a friend. Of course, he was still teaching me, leading by example. He had no opinion about his bum hips, about his tough situation. The second period of confinement to a cage did not appear to upset him. He simply sat, pondering, wagging, being. He'd accept our love and attention, breathe in deeply, catching new scents with nose-twitching curiosity and wonder, then curling up for a long, quiet nap. If that's not a lesson on how to live, I don't know what is.

Greg and I told the roommates about our romance and they

both said, "Yep, we know." So much for keeping it a secret. Still, once our relationship was public, dynamics in the house shifted. We all mourned the loss of our lovely family-of-friends vibe. We would now become a couple and two friends.

Not long after Bunker had fully healed after the second surgery, I got a phone call from Clay. "Julie?" he said. "I just wanted to know if you would please be in my wedding. Megan has picked out some dresses. She'll call you to talk about sizes and stuff. It'd be really great if you could be part of it. It would mean a lot to me," he said.

I hesitated before answering. The wedding was only six weeks away, and I wondered if I was a late addition, if my mom had forced Clay to include me. Either way, I felt as if the inclusion was a milestone. "I'd be happy to," I said, and that felt right.

I invited Greg to fly home to Ohio with me, to be my date. Everyone in the family adored Greg, noting audibly that I'd finally wised up and chosen a nice guy. Aurora and Bob already considered Greg part of the family.

I remember standing on Clay's wedding day watching the photographer snap pictures of my parents flanking my brother. He smiled, towering, at six foot four, over both my mom and dad. They were each holding one of his hands. Tears came to my eyes because, as flawed as they were, my parents tried so hard to love. They showed up when they realized that my emotional problems had become dire. How could I tell them that, despite everything, their devotion to me in my early twenties saved my life? That their belief in me was what helped me want to learn to try to love myself? The photographer paused in between shots and Clay took a deep breath. He was an adult now. Married. But I could see, perhaps for the first time, the little boy in him. I could sense the hurts he held just beneath his skin, his feelings of inadequacy, his longing for his loving but too absent father, his inability to talk to his mom, his fear of losing out to his sister and subsequent anger. I understood the solace he found in his dearest friends, a group of guys from high school who became like his brothers, who have loved, comforted, and drunk a lot of beer with him for almost thirty years now. In his desperation, Clay had made his own little makeshift family of friends. I felt immense tenderness toward him and all those guys as they smiled for the photographer. I was swept up in the joy of a wedding day. But also, I think a little part of me truly began to understand him and his ways of coping with the pain of growing up.

My job, after beginning to understand that my brother's abuse had nothing to do with me, was to try, again and again, to stop carrying it inside my own mind. It would become a lifelong mindfulness practice for me, to not think terrible things about myself, to not draw immediate, negative, judgmental, sad conclusions about every single move I made. My job is still to work my entire life to stop the self-hate. Bunker was my first and most influential teacher in this regard. He radiated contentedness and loved me no matter what. No matter how I showed up to him, no matter my mood, my energy level, no matter how I looked or smelled, he loved and adored me beyond measure. I felt the same way for him—and I'd saved him. We'd saved each other. Learning through watching his unconditional love slowly began to help me find true, compassionate self-love. It took me a long time, because healing often takes a long, meandering, circuitous route. But over time, with meditation, medication, therapy, friends, love from Greg, and lots of writing, I began to realize that the innocent, animal-loving little girl in me just wanted to love, and to be loved, and it would never be too late to give that to her.

Two months after the second surgery, Bunker and I hopped into the car and drove to Marymoor. It was the first time we'd gone there since the surgeries, since the incident with my parents and Aunt Aurora, when Bunker had fallen so badly. As we turned off of the highway and toward the park, he started prancing in the back seat, howling. "Almost there, buddy," I said, laughing, pulling into the parking lot.

I opened the car door at Marymoor and Bunker bound out of it like a spring. He ran twenty feet, then stopped to look back at me, making sure I was coming. I was fumbling with the keys, trying to lock the door. I had my running shoes on, and I zipped my keys into my jacket pocket. He ran in circles, barking, waiting for me. The way Bunker loved me, so fully, clearly, and without exception, helped me remember every day to try to bring that kind of love to myself and others in my life. I ran toward him and he took off as fast as his bionic hips could go, which was not fast at all, rather just slow enough that I could keep up with him, run right behind him, watch his funny, slightly inflexible new hips do their job. He would never run like a normal dog, and I loved him for this. Both his back legs swung to the left, and he still ran his heart out. I ran next to him, watching him leap clumsily over branches, his tongue dangling, as carefree as I'd ever seen him. We made it to the creek's edge and he stopped there, circled me three times, and then howled his deep from-the-depths howl. I squatted down next to him, held his downy soft ears in my hands, and then whispered, "No, my love. Thank *you*."

EPILOGUE: A FEW MORE THINGS I WANT YOU TO KNOW.

Four years after that romp in Marymoor, Greg and I were married in a tiny church in the woods on San Juan Island. My father walked me down the aisle and, at the last minute, I asked Clay to be a groomsman. He accepted graciously and wore a tuxedo. Bunker wore a tuxedo too and was our official ring bearer. Melissa walked him down the aisle with a baby-blue leash and he sat to my left as I promised my love to Greg. We've been married fifteen years now, and it's been hard sometimes, but he's still here, and I'm still in love, still appreciating him and his calm, his level, steady nature. We have two beautiful daughters, one who got his blue eyes, and one who got a gorgeous deep green, the color of the earth, the perfect combination of both our eyes. Those girls are our lights.

Before we were married in 2000, Chris hosted an engagement party for us at his apartment in Belltown, near downtown Seattle. He made us a beautiful video with photographs and footage of our four years together, as a couple and as four dear friends. That night, Melissa and Chris went back to his parents' house and kissed for the first time. When she called me in the morning to tell me, I screamed so loud, I'm pretty sure I shattered a window in north Seattle. They were married two years after we were. I was her maid of honor and I cried happy tears through the whole ceremony. Their reception was at a restaurant at the foot of Lake Union, where we could see our house, now fondly labeled "The Love Shack," since it had so gently fostered us all into our new loves, our new lives.

Melissa and Chris have three sons now and live in Los Angeles. We get together every chance we can get.

About my depression: There have been many times when I thought I was not depressed anymore, that I didn't need medication. I've tried to go off of antidepressants four or five times. Each time, I last under six months before I have to start taking them again. I sink down into that black place, and it is awful. I hope I've described it well enough in this story. It's a wall that closes off my mind. It's blackness. Depression is an awful voice telling me to end it all. Once, when I resumed medication, it didn't work and I had to frantically switch medications. That scared me enough to know that it's stupid to try to go off of antidepressants. Why would I? Why on earth would I gamble with my life? I remember hearing news anchor Mike Wallace say that he would always be on SSRI medication and he was simply grateful for antidepressants, because without them, he would have ended his life. I couldn't agree more. Those drugs are as essential to me as water. To whichever neurobiologists came up with SSRIs, thank you. I literally owe you my life.

I have asked Clay about some of the incidents between us as children and he said he remembered some, not all, but that he believed me, and he was sorry. His apology was both heartfelt and anticlimactic. Nothing was undone with an apology. Watching him now, as an adult myself, I know that he's not that child anymore; neither am I. He's a good man. He's a loving man. He's going to be okay. I am too. I have forgiven Clay, but I will make sure that my story is never forgotten. Too many siblings are getting hurt and hurting each other. Sibling violence is one of the last sanctioned forms of domestic abuse. Parents often say that kids just hit each other. While some aggression between siblings is inevitable, parents need to be equipped with ways to intervene and stop the fighting before it turns into serious physical, emotional, or verbal abuse. Physical fighting should never be allowed. No child should be permitted to regularly intimidate, torture, or hurt his or her sibling, because the effects of this kind of treatment will last a lifetime.

Bunker died in 2007. His entire beautiful life, I dreaded the day he would leave me. I remember crying with him on the steps of my house when he was only six because I knew he was probably half-way through his lifespan. We had moved from Seattle to Connecticut in 2000 for Greg's post-doctoral fellowship. In 2005, we moved to Berkeley for Greg's new position as a professor. By then, Bunker was nine years old, his entire face white with age. But he was still healthy. In 2006 I took him to the veterinarian for a full work-up of his elderly body, and they told me everything looked fine.

In April 2007, our oldest daughter was two, and I was seven months pregnant with our second girl. We'd bought a house, and soon after we moved in, Bunker had begun sleeping in my daughter's room. She was having bad dreams, and somehow he knew. He'd made a nest in her stuffed animals and he spent every night watching over her, ever the healer. One morning I went to her room and found an odd spot of blood on the carpet near where he slept. There was a pet food scare at the time. Food produced in China had poisoned dogs, causing massive stomach bleeding and death. I made an appointment for the veterinarian that morning and took him in while my daughter was at preschool. The vet took Bunker back for an X-ray of his abdomen and returned him to me, telling me he would be right back with the results. I was prepared for an all-clear. After all, I had taken such careful care of Bunker his whole life. Most veterinary visits were further proof that he was fine and dandy, and that I worried too much.

But this time the doctor called me into a different examination room and said, "I'm afraid I have some bad news." I buckled. All the blood rushed to my face. I remember thinking, *No, No, No.* "In the corner of the X-ray here, you can see that his lungs are almost entirely filled with cancerous tumors." *No, No, No, No.* He was eleven. I was not prepared to lose him. I was a young mother. I needed his support. I needed his consistency. I needed *him.*

The doctor left and I called my mom. I called her first because she is always there for me. Always. She answered, and I burst into sobs like the ones I had in New York. Awful, horrific sobs. "Bunker's got cancer," I cried. "The veterinarian just gave him six to eight weeks to live. Bunker's going to die, Mom!"

"Oh, my god," my mom said, and in her voice I heard tears too. I hung up and called Greg, told him, and by then everything was buzzing with terrible, awful shock. I had to pick up my two-year-old from her preschool and I needed to pull myself together. I had this beautiful little girl to care for and protect, and perhaps Bunker knew that. Perhaps he thought that his job was done. He'd cared for me and let me care for him until he knew I was going to be okay, and then he began to let go.

Those next several nights, I woke up in the middle of the night crying. Bunker had begun sleeping next to me again, because I'd asked him to. I slept with one arm draped off the bed and on his rib cage, just like I did when he was a puppy, and after his surgery, because I wanted to feel him breathing. For days, I wept something fierce. Once, when I woke up crying in the middle of the night, Greg heard me and said, "Oh, Julie, honey," scooting up behind me to hold me as we faced Bunker's unfathomable passing together. "Bunker," Greg whispered into my ear. "What a good boy."

He died ten days after the diagnosis. The veterinarian had warned me that if Bunker became lethargic, if his breathing became shallow and fast, to consider bringing him in for euthanasia. On the ninth day after the diagnosis, all of those warnings were realities. I took Bunker to the office and they put us in a room with dim light and a blanket on the floor.

But I couldn't do it. I told them I needed one more night with him. "One more night," I said. "Please. Do you think he'll make it one more night?" The vet warned me that what was happening inside Bunker's body was serious. Organs were beginning to shut down. He said that he'd seen dogs explode from the inside, dying terribly painful deaths that could've been prevented. "I can't yet. I just can't say good-bye. I'll bring him tomorrow," I said, shuffling out of the veterinarian office, feeling selfish and foolishly risky. The last thing I wanted was Bunker's suffering, but I couldn't fathom a life without him. I had twenty-four hours to make peace with the end of his life. Twenty-four hours to say good-bye. Greg took care of our daughter while I sat in our bed with Bunker, weeping over him, asking him to please watch over me after he was gone. "Please, buddy. Show me you're still with me after you're gone. Somehow. Show me I'm not alone. Thank you so much for your life. Thank you so much for helping me heal. Thank you so much for helping me see that I could be better, that I could survive, that I could make a good life for us, that letting a good man in was the best decision I could have ever made. Thank you for helping me see I wasn't totally broken after all. Thank you for showing me I was capable of healing." Through all of this, Bunker looked empty, out into nothing, until I put my face in front of his, and he saw me again, his long and beautiful feathered tail wagging weakly. My boy. Oh, my dear, dear boy.

The morning Bunker was to leave us, Greg went out and bought the best steak he could find. He grilled it on the barbecue outside and I walked Bunker gently down the stairs. He was so weak he couldn't stand, and he flopped to the ground, his front legs splayed out flat, his face sorrowful. I said, "It's time to go, Bunk. I'll be okay, buddy. I really will. You did your work. You healed me and so many other people. You were my savior, you know." I whispered this to him and his bumpy old nose sniffed the air for his last meal. Greg carefully sliced the meat into bite-sized pieces and we sat on either side of our dog and fed him one bite at a time. In thirty minutes we would take him to be euthanized. I honestly didn't know if I would have the strength to go on. I couldn't imagine my life without him. I was thirty-three now, married, with a toddler, pregnant with our second child. And I could not imagine adult life without Bunker. It was simply unfathomable.

Greg pulled up to the veterinarian's office and Bunker and I sat in the back of the car. We opened the hatch and Bunker refused to get out. He pulled back with all his might and I cried. I wept because I knew what I had to do, what he had to do. He had to leave me. And I worried I was doing the wrong thing. I was terrified I was making a mistake, but the doctor's words, *organs can explode*, ran through my mind in a terrifying mantra. I needed to protect my boy from that pain. I needed to carry him through his death, just as he had carried me through our whole lives together.

The moment the vet put the injection into Bunker's leg, when his soul left the room, every color changed. The light looked different. I wept, curled over my enormously pregnant belly. I cried over his body and the veterinarian left Greg and me to say good-bye. I lay with my head on Bunker's lifeless head whispering, "Thank you. Thank you. Thank you. Thank you so much, my love. I will miss you so much. Thank you. Thank you for my life. You will always be my angel."

When our daughter came home from preschool that afternoon and we told her Bunker had gone to heaven, she looked me straight in the eyes with those blue pools that she inherited from her father, and said, "But who will protect me from the monsters?" I wanted to ask her the same question. I wanted to say that I needed him to protect me from the monsters, too. But he had taught me that I had the capacity to protect myself. I had the capacity to choose positivity and light. I even had the capacity to help heal others. So I looked my girl in her eyes, held both her hands, and said, "Daddy and I will protect you, sweet girl. Daddy and I will be here for you every single day of your life."

A few years later, after our beautiful second daughter had reached almost three, I decided that it was time to scatter Bunker's ashes into the ocean. He loved to swim and run free, and I wanted his spirit to soar. Honestly, I wanted his essence to be free enough so that he might come back to me. I wanted a sign that he was not gone forever.

I went with three friends to Santa Cruz, where we were all tossing something into the ocean, something that meant the world to us, something we needed to let go of in order to heal. One friend, who had just endured a painful divorce, threw a heart necklace out past the breakers. Another threw a Ganesh talisman, hoping perhaps that her future held promise and love. I took Bunker's box of ashes and waded as far out as I could. I drenched my jeans, my T-shirt was sopped up to my chest, and I said out loud, "Bunker, wherever you are, I need you to know I'm still here and I still love you and I'm still grateful. I'm okay, but sometimes I still really need you and I need to know you're still here with me. How will I know?" I needed a sign. Sleeping with his ashes next to my bed had rendered no magical dreams, no beautiful appearances.

I reared back and threw the entire box of ashes out as far as I could into the Pacific. But the minute the box left my hand I regretted it. I didn't want to let Bunker go. I fought the urge to swim after it, but the water was ice cold, and I had made my decision. I walked back to shore and sat down, weeping, unsure. My friend looked out at the water and pointed.

"Look! It's coming back!" she said. I looked up, watched the box bob in the water, pushing forward with each wave toward the shore. The moon pulling the tide in. Closer. Closer. Closer. Back to land. Back to me. The box hit the beach and my friend walked to it, picked it up, and handed it to me. She set it at my feet. I grabbed it weeping, holding the sandy, wet box to my chest. I laughed, because Bunker had returned to my feet, to leaning against my shins, to telling me it would all be okay, reminding me that he's still with me, always with me, that a love like ours never dies.

Julie and Bunker in 2007

ACKNOWLEDGMENTS

I want to thank the amazing Adam Wahlberg of Think Piece Publishing for being the most incredible champion, cheerleader and trailblazer for me and for *Dog Medicine*. Adam, working with you is like working with a dear friend—a brilliant and daring dear friend. Thank you so very much for believing in this story and for partnering with me on this journey.

Endless gratitude to my beloved husband, Greg, without whom none of this would be possible. Greg, thank you for helping me create the space and time to write. You were the one who, from the beginning, encouraged me to write and not worry about all the other noise. For that I am eternally grateful. Thank you for wiping away my tears and for laughing with me in the hard times. There is nothing I cherish more than the twinkle in your eye when you're about to laugh.

To our daughters Rachel and Lucy, I love you. Remember: Always tell your truth. Always keep your heart open. And know that just like Grandma was there for me, I will be there for you every single second of your entire lives. That is what the women in our family do. We show up. Rachel, thank you for your brilliant music; it's incredible, honey. Lucy, thank you for teaching me what a gift it can be to enter every room with optimism and a smile.

To my brother, who I love, thank you for giving this story your blessing. Thank you for having the courage, as difficult as it was, to grant this story to the world. To everyone who reads this book and knows who Clay is, you know that he grew up to be a loving, caring, hilarious, fun, and generous man. Brother, to you I am grateful for your generosity in agreeing to share our difficult journey. I think it will help people.

To my mom and dad, who saved my life many times. (Remember when I wanted to know what would happen if I stuck a coat hanger in a socket?) I love you beyond measure. You guys were and are always there for me. I know now what an incredible gift that is. I am grateful that you are my parents.

To Brigid and Rob Robinson, thank you for encouraging me to pursue my dream from the beginning. To Doug and Sue Barton, thank you for inspiring me to write a book you might want to read some day. Thanks to each of you, most of all, for raising our Greg.

To Marcia Jimenez, thank you for showing me that my connection to animals and nature wasn't weird or wrong. To Rich and Adriane and Corinne, I love you guys. Thank you for taking me in as one of your own. It brought me such solace during a time I needed it. Ross, you're the best bro-cuz anyone could ask for.

To Grandma and Grandpa Hill, I love you and I feel you with me. I keep your picture next to my desk. Thank you for my beloved father. You raised a spectacular human being.

To Grandma and Grandpa Houdek, thank you for showing me what family feels like. With all its ups and downs and twists and turns, the one thing I've always been able to count on is the smell of Grandma's house and warm houska bread or spritz cookies. Thank you for the strength of all the women in our family.

Linda, Rich, Angie, and Tina, thank you for sharing your dog love with me. I love you all.

To Tom, Whitney, Mele, Koa, and Nanea, thank you for your support. Whitney, your help was invaluable at the end of this process and I'm grateful.

To my chosen family: Erik and Michelle. You were Bunker's second parents. Thank you. Michelle, you taught me what real friendship felt like. I am grateful to you for that. Erik, you're an inspiration and I admire you beyond measure. Navigating the first few years of real adulthood with both of you was one of my life's greatest gifts. To Henry, Shane, and Ben, I love you boys. You make me proud. Otto and Dudley, you're good dogs.

To my Vermont College of Fine Arts sisters, Dawn Haines and Robin Oliveira: I adore you both. Dawn, this book would not be here without you, without your wise eye, your careful editing, your knowledge of sentence and structure. Thank you for your expertise and your friendship. Robin, thank you for blazing the trail, for inspiring me with your brilliant books, your vast skill, and your unending support. Thank you also for answering the phone and helping me breathe through hysterical tears—more than once.

Thank you to Lisa Grantham. Thank you for your friendship and for building the bridge between Adam Wahlberg and me. For that I will be forever grateful. Thank you also for affirming that friends who like to stay in can be just as fun and hilarious as friends always out on the town.

To Robin MacArthur and Anne Kelley Conklin, for your careful edit, your caring words, your kindness. To Karen Lynch for taking so much time to help me craft this story when it was still in early stages.

To all my teachers at Kenyon College, Southern Connecticut State University (SCSU), Vermont College of Fine Arts, and Esalen Institute: P.F. Kluge, Tim Parrish, Vivian Shipley, Rosalyn Amenta, Sue William Silverman, David Jauss, Larry Sutin, Pamela Painter, Laurie Alberts, Steve Almond, Cheryl Strayed, Pam Houston, Samantha Dunn, and Alan Heathcock—thank you for your wisdom, encouragement, and inspiration. To the folks in the SCSU Women's Studies and English departments, thank you for championing me. I'm so grateful. To the wonderful people at Vermont College of Fine Arts, you have created an oasis of safety and creativity and brilliance. Thank you for fostering me through your beautiful program. It changed my life.

To all of you Esalen writers: I adore every ounce of all of you. Thank you and love to Lisa Russ, Melanie Simonich, Karen Lynch,

Amy Sterne, Francesca Kaplan Grossman, Amy Kortuem, Lalé Shafaghi, Hilary Tellesen, and Sarah Pape.

Endless gratitude to the beloved Laurie Wagner and all those brave souls writing their hearts out around her sacred table at 27 Powers: Keep writing as poorly as possible because the most brilliant writing flows from your moving pens.

To my teacher Illana Berger: You were the first one to truly affirm for me, as an adult, that my connection to nature was a gift. Thank you for your unfailing wisdom, your friendship, your love. To Jennifer Brault for your friendship. I love you, soul sister. To my sacred women's group—I love you guys. Thank you for taking the risk with me to be 100 percent real with each other.

To my Piedmont friends, thank you for your support and excitement and for joining me along the way. I would list you all, but I'd be terrified of forgetting someone. You know who you are.

To Ryan Scheife, who took a sixteen-year-old photograph and created the most stunning book cover I've ever seen. Wow. Thank you. Your patience and skill are beyond measure.

To all the dogs who came before: Bunker Hill the 1st, Sam, Midnight, Ebony, Blarney, Cinder, Bogey, Rocky, and Ben. You are all my angels.

To Bunker. Thank you. I miss you. I love you. This book is for you. You brought so much healing into the lives of so many. I carry you with me. Always. Sometimes I play old home movies of you just to hear you howl. Thank you for loving me so completely, Bunka-doo. You taught me everything.

Finally, to my current dog, Jackson, a rescue mutt who is eight years old but as hyper as a puppy. You may not bring the kind of dog medicine I'm used to—you may be a pain in my butt sometimes—but I am slowly learning that even you bring important medicine. Thank you for lying in the dog bed just to the left of my desk as I wrote much of this story. I know you were working some kind of magic. You're a good boy. I love you. Walk time?